Educating Young Children ... Sociological Interpretations

Educating
Young Children
. . . Sociological
Interpretations

EDITH W. KING
University of Denver

WM. C. BROWN COMPANY PUBLISHERS
Dubuque, Iowa

Selections from *You and Me* by Charlotte Zolotow reprinted with permission of the Macmillan Company from *Social Studies:Focus on Active Learning Series.* Copyright © 1971 by the Macmillan Company.

Selections from "How Children See Society" first appeared in *New Society* (Nov. 19, 1970), the weekly review of social science, 128 Long Acre, London WC2.

Selections from Schools Council Working Paper 39, *Social Studies 8-13* (Evans/Methuen Educational, London, 1971, and distributed in the U.S.A. and Canada by Citation Press) are reproduced by permission from School Council.

Several of the Children's pictures were photographed and used by courtesy of Robert Keyser.

Consulting Editor

Joseph Frost
University of Texas, Austin

Copyright © 1973 by Wm. C. Brown Company Publishers

Library of Congress Catalog Card Number: 72—91812

ISBN 0—697—06035—7

Printed in the United States of America

For the members of the

EDUCATIONAL RESOURCES CENTER

Boulder, Colorado

Contents

Foreword

In 1971, Edith King's *The World: Context for Teaching in the Elementary School* was presented to educators. The theme of this book was developing worldmindedness in young children—a theme drawing energy from dynamic social forces in contemporary living that are propelling individuals into a world culture. Taking into account the dangers of premature conceptualization, the author promoted the concept of "spaceship earth" through the integration of the social sciences and the arts—all within a humanistic framework.

Now, Professor King brings sociological theory to bear upon early childhood education—preschool through primary. The socialization of young children, more specifically, the development of positive concepts of self and others, is the primary focus of the present volume. Sociological theory, translated through case illustrations and concrete implications for classroom practice, make this work a valuable aid to teachers.

Cast in the framework of recent events, this is a bold book. The latter sixties was a time of great emphasis upon "cognitive development" of young children. A great deal of criticism was directed toward the "social orientation" of early childhood programs. Time and experience have taught the futility of attempted estrangement of the social and cognitive dimensions. The fundamental principle that major components of human development are interrelated and interdependent has survived the tests of the sixties and, as this book demonstrates for the social domain, sophistication has been added to survival. The enhancement of young children's concepts of self and others is not a haphazard task but one for which adults must provide skillful, creative guidance from a scientific base. This book charts the course for this process.

JOE L. FROST
Consulting Editor

Preface

Life In Classrooms, The Culture of the Classroom, The Experience of Schooling, the Unstudied Curriculum,—titles of books dealing with contemporary problems in education are changing along with their focus and content. Suddenly we are concerned with the social, emotional, and affective aspects of those participating in the educational enterprise. The content of the curriculum is taking a back stage position, while front and center before the footlights the socio-cultural aspects of the teaching-learning process are presented. My choice of theatrical terminology is not by chance, but carefully calculated to reflect another new direction, this one from the discipline of sociology. Here then, is seen the thrust and concern of this book, the application of new directions in sociology—dramaturgic sociology, symbolic interactionism, the inspection of everyday life, the taken-for-granted daily activities—to the educative process.

More specifically, I focus on the early childhood classroom and the culture of childhood because I feel that the years three through eight are the crucial years for the developing personality and intellect of the child. Sociology has much to offer educators and particularly early childhood educators, yet little research and writing have been devoted to the application of sociological theory in the teaching of young children.

This book then is for students preparing to teach young children and for those already involved in classrooms of young children. The materials presented on these pages view the young child's classroom as a social arena. This book looks at the socialization process in the early childhood setting and considers how children are stigmatized and discredited even early in life. Beyond the sociological investigation into the young child's classroom, school, family group, and neighborhood, this volume considers the child in a world society. The implications for educating the child to function in global society as well as considerations of face to face interactions are drawn from classical sociological theory. The major contribution that sociological theory can make to those concerned with the education of young children has been overlooked for too long. This book attempts to fill some of this gap in the literature. It is hoped that other educational sociologists will note the effort expended here to bring sociological theory to bear upon primary education and add to the writings and research in this newly recognized area—the sociology of early childhood education.

A teacher just naturally turns to her students to state how much they have contributed to the writing of her book—this teacher is no exception. The students in my courses at the University of Denver and their students in the public schools in addition to the early childhood programs represent a multiplier effect that has generated many inputs for this volume. But I must not disregard my colleagues in education, sociology, and the broader purview of the social sciences who have interacted with me offering advice, suggestions, and contributions for the manuscript. Finally, I cite with specific mention my consulting editor, Joe Frost, of the University of Texas at Austin, whose encouragement, support, and thoughtful criticism of the manuscript were essential to the successful completion of this work.

EDITH W. KING

Educating Young Children . . . Sociological Interpretations

chapter 1

The Young Child's Classroom as a Social Arena

Over the years the main thrust in education, elementary school or secondary, has consistently emphasized the cognitive *content* of the curriculum. When do we begin *reading*? In kindergarten? In first grade? When are the children "ready"? How much time should we spend on *arithmetic*? There has to be *science* in the curriculum. Do not forget *art* and *music* and *social science* and *physical education*! Yet the whole area of the affective and the emotive within the curriculum, which in recent writings has been termed the "hidden" curriculum, the "unstudied" curriculum, the *culture* of the classroom, has been treated less intensively. Especially in teacher training programs, but also in in-service workshops and refresher courses, the emphasis has been on beefing up the teachers' knowledge of content in a particular area or of informing parents, administrators, the board of education or the public about new developments in technological expertise rather than in exploring the less concrete and far more controversial areas of affective domains in teaching and learning.

Occasionally there has been a school district's program, a university offering, a federally-funded institute or workshop that delved into the intricacies of children's social and emotional life, but this type of educational project is the exception. The majority of training programs still concentrate on the cognitive, concrete content of the curriculum in schools and universities. Now and then in the educational literature a book or pamphlet is noted for offering insights and commentary on this affective, feeling level of the educational experience, but it appears as more part of a passing fad than a sustained interest in the educational training of teachers and administrators.

It is the purpose of this book to explore the literature currently available on the social nature of the young child's classroom, to provide examples and illustrations of how this information can be applied in practice, and finally to encourage teachers and administrators of programs for young children to become aware of the implications of the young child's classroom as a social arena. The underlying effort here is to reveal the possibilities inherent in the application of the more recent developments in "dramaturgic sociology" with early childhood education.

"Dramaturgic" sociology is an offshoot of earlier symbolic interactionist theories. It emphasizes a concern with how social "reality" is created in day-to-day activities by the use of "dramatic" devices such as costumes, gestures, back-stage preparations, rehearsals, etc. One of the foremost modern writers in this area of concern is Erving Goffman. His writings have given the dramaturgic thrust of sociology today special implications for teachers and administrators of programs for young children. This is a new venture in early childhood education, although writings and research in the sociology of the self and explorations in self-psychology have been part of the social scientific scene for several decades.

Fig. 1.1. Drawing by a six-year-old, Birmingham, England—"School." His teacher remarked that paradoxically there are no boards with sums on them anywhere in the classroom. Note the child turning on the TV set, lower right. Television is a major learning facility in British primary schools. (Courtesy of Shirley Meighan Tanhouse Infants School, Birmingham, England.)

THE CLASSROOM AS A SOCIAL ARENA

What do we seek when we ask to view the young child's classroom as a social arena? One aspect of such a concern is the general climate in the room or in the school totally. Are students smiling and happy? Does one occasionally hear laughter or chuckles? Or is the general tone one of graveness, solemnity, scowls and frowns and downcast eyes? Though we tend to think of schools, classrooms, or casual groupings of young children as "happy places" full of warmth, dynamic movement, and smiling children engaged in play, this is not necessarily what is actually taking place. Nor is it necessarily what may be taking place in the individual classrooms of those schools either. So in dealing with social climate we can evaluate the general atmosphere of classroom or school, the overall social climate of openness or closedness and of interpersonal warmth or coldness. There are a variety of terms that can be used for such assessments and these will be described later.

Beyond the general tone of the group setting, there is the special and particular climate that surrounds each member of the group, each child or adult in the classroom. Here we can ask such questions as: Is the individual secure or threatened? Does he feel this way momentarily or continually? Is the individual a valued member of the group or a marginal person, used by others or trying to use them? Can the individuals in the group communicate with each other or are there barriers to interpersonal relations? Are there partial channels of communication between only some members of the group which are not open to others of the group? The analysis of the classroom as a social arena is a complex and intricate study, as these questions begin to show.

We need to ask also about the quality of the relationships in this social arena containing young children and the adults that care for them. Are these relationships—which stem from power and status positions— benign or are they vicious? Or can there be components of both these aspects of power relationships in the dealings and ministrations of adults with young children? The issue is not one-sided. We must examine how children struggle to exert power and not assume power as the teacher's exclusive right. Certainly we have evidence in the psychological literature of the vicious nature of children's interactions with other children. How does duration, timing, lasting effect or temporary impact affect the power relation to render the interaction benign or vicious? Some action that might traumatize a little boy, for example, might roll off some little girl!

When considering abstract theory, it is helpful to present concrete examples. The following report of a fifteen-minute observation in a classroom of young children, with interpretive notes, provides illustrations of many of the points stated above.

The Classroom Setting: It is early in the school year, a crisp, sunny autumn morning. The new second graders (seven-year olds) file into the highly organized classroom, filling their assigned seats in the neat rows very quietly. Each child is expected to fold his hands together, lips still, and face forward with eager look, awaiting the teacher's signal that roll call is about to begin. The teacher, a petite, attractive woman, in her early thirties, makes it clear she will wait until every child is "ready"—hands folded, no talking, eyes front. The children obey, although there is some rustling of coins and a few whispers as a loose nickel is retrieved. Roll call is taken. The lunch count is made.

The Classroom Drama: The teacher then brings out a small box from her desk. It has a colorful emblem on it. She asks the children if they remember what the box is for. One girl raises her hand and is called on by the teacher. The child responds that this is the UNICEF box to collect contributions for children *all over the world* who are not as "fortunate" as we are. (One begins to think that this teacher has her children as neatly programmed as the chairs, desks, and materials in the classroom.) Now the teacher asks, "And who has brought a contribution for our UNICEF box this morning?"

The same girl jumps up quickly, and rushes up to the teacher waving a dollar bill. "I have a dollar!" she declares proudly. The teacher then requests the child to write on the blackboard with the chalk the amount of her contribution, $1.00. The child does so, and the teacher turns back to the class, saying, "Very fine Gail, you brought a whole dollar contribution to our box and you wrote the amount correctly on the board. Now who else has a contribution today?"

Some shuffling and a little hurried whispering takes place. Then a boy at the rear of the room raises his hand and is recognized by the teacher. "I have a nickel?" he says rather wistfully, as though he expected the teacher to reject his contribution after the magnificent one before. "Very good, Jim, come up to the front of the room and drop your *nickel* [emphasized] in our box and write down on the board your contribution under Gail's. Boys and girls, we will see if Jim can add the amounts correctly and you do it with him at your seat."

Slowly Jim approaches the front of the room and places his contribution in the box, then proceeds to write the five cents on the board under the dollar and attempts to do the addition. The teacher continues to solicit the children for money to put in the UNICEF box, but no other volunteer contributions.

Should There Be Applause? In analyzing the implications and ramifications of this brief classroom drama, several attributes of the dramatis personae should be further described. The children in this class, the seven-year-olds, come from a range of backgrounds and socioeconomic levels. Of the 33 children in the class, four are blacks, bussed in from a distant part of the city to officially integrate this class and the school. The majority of the children come from upper-middle–class families whose parents are professionally employed or owners of businesses. The affluence in the homes of the majority of the children is reflected in the objects and games they brought for the "Show and Tell" time that followed the "charity" episode described above. One has to ask to what degree a climate of materialism is being developed in this group of seven-year-olds by a seemingly well-meaning teacher?

Further, the teacher appeared very smug and self-satisfied that she had creatively developed an *arithmetic lesson* out of a mundane activity like contributing to a charity. One wonders how affronted she would be if her school principal asked her to contribute to the United Fund or some other such charitable function publicly in front of the school staff? It can almost be assumed that she would call this an invasion of her personal privacy to be as charitable as she chose. Yet this woman did not hesitate to place the seven-year-olds in her classroom in an embarassing and socially difficult situation, indicating that, as is frequently the case, adults do not consider that young children can be socially sensitive to exploitive situations.

Here then, is an example of how power and status relationships in a classroom of young children can sometimes function to create malicious results unleashed by a well-intentioned, professional, middle-class white teacher attempting to inculcate in her children the values of charitable actions together with the important content learning of addition in mathematics!

If during the recent troubled years in public education teachers needed to be aware of the social and emotional connotations of what they taught in the classroom, then today—with the stepping-up of integration, the controversies over bussing for desegregation, the influences of the community upon school policy, and the numerous other forces coming to play upon the public school—such awareness is imperative. One does not simply teach reading, arithmetic, science, music, art, and so on to children. The very content, the words, the subjects chosen, the method by which they are presented all have subtle and indirect meanings to various members of the early childhood class. The teacher must internalize this knowledge and use it to guide every action. The attitude that children of four, five, six, or seven years are just too young to "know the difference" is a false and cruel assumption.

Since we have presented an illustration of behavior bordering on the vicious by a teacher of young children, let the following description of a positive climate in a classroom of young children stand to counter-balance the first episode.

The Classroom Setting: It is a cold, dark, and snowy day in midwinter. In this classroom of five- and six-year-olds movement is free and easy. Children come and go between interest centers that have been placed casually, but with much care and study set up for their use. The class membership is small today, only 12 children, because a number are absent with colds or other illnesses. The class is also limited in size because it is part of a demonstration early-childhood center. The children in the class come from diverse backgrounds— black, white, Hispano—from lower income families and from affluent ones. The mixture includes normal children and physically handicapped or emotionally disturbed youngsters. The philosophy of the school is not to segregate young children in homogeneous tracks but to attempt a blending of various backgrounds for more democratic and successful learning for all children.

The Classroom Drama: Six children are standing around a low table at one end of the room. On the tables are cooking ingredients. Just above the table, tacked to the wall, is a chart story. It is actually a recipe, written in large letters and numbers titled "Cupcakes." The children are manipulating the ingredients—flour, baking powder, sugar, salt and the implements—measuring spoons, cups, bowls, a mixing spoon. The teacher sits off to the side, mainly watching the children but reacting to their questions. "Is this stirred enough?" one boy asks. "Look! Jonathan spilled some of the stuff," a girl remarks. Two boys with paper baker hats on shout, "We want to mix, it's our turn now," and they both proceed to grab for the mixing spoon. The teacher calmly directs the taking of turns for the mixing. She reacts to the spills with a normal tone of voice, noting for the children that flour usually spills a little for anyone who is mixing. To the questions of how much salt or how much baking powder to use, this teacher responds with, "Look at our recipe on the wall, what does it say?" The two five-year-olds can read the numbers and they react with confident tones, "One half a teaspoon of salt!"

The batter is mixed and ready to be poured in the pans. Two children other than the mixers take turns filling the pans with the batter. Then the teacher says, "Who wants to go downstairs to put the cupcakes in the oven?" A chorus of "I's" and "Me's" is the response. "Be sure to read the chart and see how long we have to bake them," she notes, as the children take up the cupcake tins full of batter and prepare to leave the room.

There Should Be Applause! How different the social atmosphere, the climate of the classroom in this room of young children compared to that in the first classroom described. The curriculum, the opportunities for learning, are organized so that the child can be self-teaching, self-learning. The environment is so programmed that the child can find the answers readily. The adult in the situation provides guidance and support, not autocratic directing, for fulfillment of the teacher-chosen tasks. In this classroom the surroundings say "touch me," "use me," not "you will be punished if you get out of your seat." This teacher is not afraid to trust children and their capacity to utilize materials and tools wisely with care and concern to achieve their purposes.

To return to our concepts of power and status relationships as benign or vicious forces at work in classrooms of young children, we can see how the adult, the teacher, can exercise structure and discipline, provide organization, without creating an atmosphere of malevolence and distrust. Young children in groups do need the support and security of boundaries, rules, routines, and regularity, yet within this there needs to be recognition of individual differences and individual rights.

Now let us turn to some of the theorists—sociologists and educators—who have examined the classroom as a social arena. In presenting theories and concepts, we will discuss their implications for teaching young children.

FROM THE 1930s: THE WORK OF WILLARD WALLER

In what has been labeled a "classic" book, Willard Waller, a faculty member at Pennsylvania State who was teaching educational sociology in the 1930s, described and delineated in depth and detail that "other" curriculum, the hidden curriculum of the school. It is ironic that over forty years ago a talented social scientist was focusing on the very aspects of schooling that today have become so crucial to writers and observers of the educational scene.

In the introduction to the 1965 edition of Waller's *The Sociology of Teaching* (first published in 1932), Cole Brembeck writes this about the book:

> In a sense Waller makes every teacher an educational sociologist. He takes the commonplace events in the human life of the school and its surroundings, things many teachers might tend to overlook, and holds them up for examination like a good teacher does. He turns them around and inside out, he describes and relates them to people like teachers, students, and parents, he places them in the larger context of many schools, many teachers, students and parents, and suddenly the routine life of the school takes on excitement and magic, the gifts of insight and perspective.[1]

In *The Sociology of Teaching* Waller looks at the nature of the school as a social organism and its role in the social process. He views the relationship of the school to the community from a broad stance, and then focuses on specific aspects of teachers in the community as they relate to parents and to their students. Particularly in Waller's interpretations of school life, where he describes the separate culture of school with its

---

1. Willard Waller, *The Sociology of Teaching*. (New York: John Wiley & Sons, Inc. 1965, Science Edition paperback), front matter.

ceremonies, crowd psychology, and primary groups among school children, are his insights pertinent and timely. His chapter on teaching as institutionalized leadership has many implications for those working with young children, as does his commentary on attitudes and roles in classroom situations. In the next few pages we will draw out from Waller's writings the observations and insights that have particular meaning and relevance for teaching young children.

Earlier in this chapter it was noted that not only should teachers be aware of the group climate, they should also realize that each individual in the classroom is immersed in his own version of that social atmosphere. Waller states this eloquently when he writes, "Each child has a position that is his and his only, and views life with unique perspective." [2]

In an often quoted passage he describes how the young child's mental life develops by a series of "Aha moments," moments of insight, when suddenly, perhaps intuitively, the child makes connections in his thinking between objects and words, or interrelations between objects, and objects and ideas.

The concept of "Aha moments" fits in well with Piagetian theory. As one views the stages of mental growth that Piaget delineates: the sensori-motor stage, when the child is touching, feeling, exploring his physical environment; the pre-operational stage with its components of intuitive thinking leading the child to jump to conclusions about his physical environment that might not be so in fact; the stage of concrete operations built upon more extensive acquisition of language and broader experience (now the child can classify objects, perform seriation and enumeration); and then the final stage labeled "formal operations" (usually occuring at upper elementary grade levels about ages 11 or 12 on, and characterized by mastery of mathematical, relational, and deductive thinking), the "Aha moment" can be constructed as that instant when a young child can move in his thinking about an object or an idea from one stage to the next higher one in mental development. The following anecdote exemplifies this:

> Three kindergarten children are seated at a table with their teacher. The teacher has by her some bunches of plastic flowers, red and yellow roses and white daisies, and some plastic vases in which the flowers can be arranged easily. The teacher gives each child a vase and an equal amount of the plastic flowers. First she asks the children what they have. They all reply that they have some plastic flowers and a vase. Then the teacher requests the children to find all the roses and put them in the vase—just the roses. "Count the roses," she says.

---

2. Ibid., p. 36.

The children count—ten roses, two red and eight yellow. Next the children are told to take all the roses out of the vase and make a bouquet, this time in the vase with just the yellow roses. The three children do so. Again, the roses in the vase are counted—eight yellow roses.

Now the teacher asks the three children, "Are there more roses or more yellow roses?" The five-year-old girl replies by pointing to the yellow roses in the vases. The teacher verbalizes for her, saying, "Oh, there are more yellow roses than roses altogether?" The child nods her head, yes. But one of the boys shakes his head, no. His eyes light up and he picks up the two red roses from the table and places them in the vase with the yellow roses, saying, "No, there are more roses, altogether, red and yellow, than just the yellow roses, 'cause they are all roses." The child has experienced an "Aha moment" in his thinking.

This five-year-old boy has begun to move in his thinking into the Piagetian stage of concrete operations where he can classify objects from a general class (roses) into subclasses (red and yellow roses). The five-year-old girl still depends on the impression that when the yellow roses are massed together, it looks like there are more, so there must be more yellow ones than roses altogether. Since the others are spread out away from the main group, she wouldn't classify them as roses.[3]

Working with young children is rewarding because they indicate so expressively by facial and body reactions, as well as in words, when an "Aha moment" has occurred in their thinking and intellectual development.

Intellectual development occurs so subtly that adults easily forget the "Aha moments" in their life. What seems an obvious and simple observation to a grownup, can be a giant intellectual step for a child. This is part of what forms the barrier between the young and those who are matured. Waller describes this in a passage that prophesies the generation gap struggle of the fifties and sixties:

> Age is not the only factor that separates people who nominally drink of the same cultural stream from actual community of culture. Mental ability, education, subtle differences of interests and of personality may likewise sort people into cultural pigeonholes. So completely is the individual immersed in the culture of his own age and social level that he

3. Related during a demonstration by Celia Stendler Lavatelli (the teacher in the story) at the University of Denver, Phipps House Conference in Early Childhood Education, July 6, 1971. Dr. Lavatelli was demonstrating her Piagetian materials with kindergarten children to Head Start, and Early Childhood teachers (Early Childhood Education Programs, American Science and Engineering, Boston, Mass., 1971). See also, C. S. Lavatelli, *A Piagetian Approach to an Early Childhood Curriculum* (Boston: American Science and Engineering, 1971).

often has difficulty in realizing that any other kind of culture exists. He is separated by invisible walls from those about him who follow different gods. Persons living in different segments of our culture, as determined by age and life situation, may find difficulty in communicating with each other or in understanding each other at all.[4]

When looking at the separate culture of the school, Waller holds up for examination the folkways and traditions that grow up in every school and among groups of school children. Although he draws his examples mainly from groups of high school or university students, he notes that certain folkways (such as the practice of riding one's bicycle to school when in the elementary grades but never riding it when in high school) are characteristic of the age-grading effects on customs of school children. "Membership in the older group implies repudiation of the folkways of the younger group. No one more foolish than . . . the college boy wearing a high school letter!" [5]

These observations about folkways among children certainly have their counterparts among young children. The example can be seen in kindergarten boys who will no longer play in the doll corner, as they did in nursery or pre-school, and insist on the blocks, trucks, and "male"-oriented toys in the kindergarten room. Waller also discusses the importance of tradition in the school culture. Even early childhood classes have traditions that function to provide solidarity and cohesiveness for the group.

One enterprising teacher of kindergarteners adopted a high school tradition of the area to elect a "head boy" and a "head girl." These were traditionally (in the high school setting) all-around outstanding students, good in the academic, social, and athletic aspects of school life. The kindergarten teacher developed a criteria for assessing who would be rated as a "head boy" or "head girl." The children in the kindergarten class nominated likely candidates and judged if their merits and performance met these criteria. When a child passed the standards and was elected as "head boy" or "head girl," the child received a special badge to wear and was honored accordingly by his classmates. The titles were eagerly sought after in this kindergarten and provided a strong incentive for individual as well as group merit and recognition.

Waller has some cogent advice for teachers of students at all ages. He suggests that if one has two highly verbal and aggressive members in a class, they should be seated at opposite ends of the room. They can carry on their interchanges from opposite sides of the room so that other children in the class will be more apt to enter in the discussions. This encourages a general discussion of issues. If you seat the two highly verbal

---

4. *The Sociology of Teaching*, p. 106.
5. Ibid., p. 110.

individuals next to each other, the sociologist observes, they are more likely to carry on in a personal and disruptive manner.[6] Yet he notes that "Ultimately, education must individualize. And in the ideal school every member of the educative group will participate as a complete person, and not as the part of a person that makes a part of a crowd." [7]

Where Waller describes teaching as institutionalized leadership, he provides understanding for those working with young children today. He points out that in institutional leadership the leader has been established by a process other than the one used to pick the personal leader. The institutionalized leader steps into a situation already prepared for him. The school depends almost entirely upon institutional leadership. Where personal leadership is present, prestige is necessary and usually flows from the personal characteristics of the leader. He has been chosen for these reasons. But in institutional leadership prestige is attached to the office or the position. In both types of leadership social distance is required, but in institutionalized leadership social distance is essential. In the case of the school and the teacher, it would be ludicrous if the leader (the teacher) were discovered to be totally inept and unqualified for the position. There are fascinating stories and novels, films and plays about faltering leaders, including teachers, who create all manner of ruses and disguises to cover their inadequacies. But what about the teacher of young children? It is often thought that it does not take much intellectual ability, let alone leadership qualities, to teach young children. A babysitting function is frequently the attitude displayed by others—"Oh, she's only a nursery school teacher"—indicating that the teacher is not bright enough to teach *older* children.

How false is this attitude! It must be dispelled and replaced with an accurate picture of the nature of leadership and teaching in early childhood education. The teacher of young children can maintain social distance from her students merely by physical size and strength alone, as well as by intellectual and emotional maturity, but it is gifted teachers, or institutional leaders in this case, who can put themselves imaginatively in the place of the four-, five-, or six-year-old to empathize with the child and understand his problems, his successes, or his anguish.

Further, Waller goes on to point out that the school as an institution practices dominance and subordination, which in the language of the school is called "discipline." The teachers have means for keeping their students in line. Here the dominant personality enters into the relationship with his whole personality, or a large portion of himself, while the subordinated personality gives but a small part of himself. Yet for the

6. Ibid., p. 163.
7. Ibid., p. 174.

subordinate, the student, punishment has real value in that it serves to define the situation. As Waller says, "It puts the student in the way of distinguishing clearly the permitted and the not-permitted, the right and the wrong within the complex social situation of the school." [8]

After a graduate student in educational sociology observed first-hand the application of Waller's concepts of dominance and subordination as discipline in a classroom of young children, she wrote:

> Discipline in a classroom of children has got to be maintained no matter how progressive or open the style of teaching. Discipline in this class-room is conducted in a subdued but unmistakable tone. During the reading period a look between the teacher and students ended or cur-tailed distracting activities. A word sufficed elsewhere. Discipline in a class-wide activity is more vocal, however. It is geared to the student's sense of fair play and sharing of the responsibility for the operation of the classroom. It also appeals to their considerateness of other people. For example:
>
> During a class discussion Darrell dropped a small button he was playing with. Darla lunged for it, picked it up and offered it to Darrell who took it rather gruffly from her. Darla's anger broke out and she spoke to Darrell very loudly. The teacher ordered her to her seat with words of criticism to this effect: "Darla, there is no reason that this entire class should have to be distracted from their lesson because you and Darrell have a problem. Whatever it is must be resolved by you two. Please have more consideration for the rest of us."
>
> During another discussion two girls were conducting their own talk while the teacher was speaking. She quickly ended that distraction by a look and a "Pardon me, was I interrupting you?"
>
> I have noted the success of this second technique as it is used every-day, but sparingly and very effectively. Regarding the first incident, I found myself wanting to defend Darla for Darrell had been dropping his little toy on the ground continuously through the lesson and had actually been quite rough and rude in taking it back from Darla. Later the teacher explained to me that her reprimanding pupils was never the result of one instance of disruptive behavior. In Darla's case it seemed when she was called upon in class to answer questions her voice was inaudible. But in other situations she is liable to have a very loud and distracting pitch to her voice.
>
> There are many theories of discipline among educational sociologists. The fear motive seems to be the most prevalent method discernible in maintaining appropriate behavior. Related to this is Waller's theory of subordination and domination in the classroom. In all aspects of school life the main issue is the asserting of domination by the teacher over the subordinate students. Over and against this is the affectionate relation-ship between teacher and student in a democratic classroom. In between lies the difficult middle ground of treating the pupils as responsible human beings where possible and yet being able to bring down a strong hand

---

8. Ibid., p. 200.

upon them for undesirable and disruptive behavior. It becomes a matter of effective and efficient domination by the teacher where necessary and for a specific reason.

The young children in the class I observed when reprimanded or disciplined, seemed to understand why they were reprimanded. They were always told how inconsiderate they have been. The effective use of group loyalty was observed. They had not simply broken an arbitrary regulation, they had been unkind to their friends. Of course, anyone being reprimanded is always the focus of attention and those other pairs of eyes focused upon the culprit must certainly help to reinforce the effect of punishment. In lesser infractions of the rules merely a look from the teacher sufficed to remind the student to watch his behavior.[9]

Should teachers of young children feel a laissez-faire attitude toward enforcing all rules with the children? Waller cogently states that: "Rules may be emasculated by attrition through setting up exceptions which at first seem harmless to the established order but when translated into precedent are found to destroy some parts of it altogether. One value of experience in teaching is that it gives the teacher an understanding of precedents. A trivial favor to Johnny Jones becomes a ruinous social principle when it is made a precedent." [10] Even three-year-olds are socially aware enough to note that "If David can ride the trike in the play-yard before Milk and Cookies Time, why can't I ride it now?" It takes an astute and attentive teacher, an institutionalized leader, to use Waller's terminology, to handle the myriad of discipline problems in the early childhood classroom, as in the total school setting.

Finally Waller writes with insight and clarity on the topic of attitudes and roles in the classroom situation. He characterizes a role as a social attitude reflected back upon the individual either actually or in his imagination.[11] He sees the playing of roles and the acquisition of behavior patterns as being the central process in the development of personality. Examining the roles which students, teachers, administrators, ancillary personnel, and parents play in the educational setting is a fascinating study. We will delve more deeply in chapter 2 into this whole realm of roles, interpersonal interaction, and the background on which the social drama is played when we take up the work and writings of Erving Goffman. Even so, recognition must be given to the fact that over 40 years ago Willard Waller was considering some of these very same dynamic processes in the school and in the educational institution.

The Sociology of Teaching contains, at the end of selected chapters, various projects and suggestions for studies of the culture of the school

---

9. Linda Pohle, "Microethnography in the Elementary School" (unpublished study, Educational Sociology, School of Education, University of Denver, June, 1970), pp. 13 and 14.
10. *The Sociology of Teaching*, p. 196.
11. Ibid., p. 321.

and for interpretations of life in schools. Some of these projects are listed here for your consideration. They were chosen for their pertinence to early childhood education and their application to the social atmosphere in classrooms of young children in the seventies.

Study some community conflict which has resulted in a change of school policy.

Make a list of the suggestions publicly offered for the improvement of the schools during a given period. How far do these represent the activities of conflict groups?

Begin a street-corner conversation with a stranger. Lead him to express himself as freely as possible. Midway in the conversation, remark that you are a school teacher of young children. Record the results. Repeat the observation. Interpret.

Record the comments made by members of a community about teachers, particularly teachers of young children, such as "the kindergarten teacher." Interpret.

Have a group of teachers living in a small community make lists of their closest friends, noting occupations. Do the same for a larger community. What conclusions can you draw?

Take notes on the shop talk of teachers. How much of it concerns the "universe of children's attitudes and values"?

Analyze the hold upon the community of some prominent teacher who is secure in his position.

Determine by questioning teachers and by study of grading or evaluation whether teachers more easily establish cordial relationships with morning or afternoon classes.

Analyze the reaction of different classes to slight mishaps, such as stumbling, etc., of the teacher. Show type reactions which go with different kinds of rapport between student and teacher. Devise informal tests for teachers upon this basis. How must the teacher pass off mishaps?

Give instances of fashion in the school.

Give examples of remarks or gestures which come to symbolize humor in the school.

Study the political process in a self-governing play group. How are decisions arrived at? How is discipline enforced? What is ambition?

Study the play group relationships of a precocious child who is considerably ahead of his own age group in school. What problems does his social life present?

Make a case study of a younger brother. How complete is the younger brother's exclusion from the older brother's play associations, and what is its effect upon the younger brother's personality?

Make a case study of a boy who likes to play with younger children.

Make a study of "fighting words" in a group of young boys.

Analyze the laughter of teacher and students in a particular class for the light it sheds upon the rapport between teacher and student.

Study the use of students' first names by teachers. Analyze in terms of social distance. Does faculty practice affect student usage? [12]

---

12. Ibid., pp. 14, 30, 174, 188, 316.

WALLER REVISITED: THE WRITINGS OF PHILIP JACKSON

We have remarked that in recent years a major theme in educational literature has become a concern with the social atmosphere in the school and in the classroom. As the cognitive area of learning appeared more and more manageable through technology and in educational research with the use of computers, the unknown variable, those "aleatory factors" in sociological terminology, arose again and again to cloud the results of carefully designed research studies in learning and cognition. This led contemporary educators, educational psychologists, social psychologists, and sociologists to investigate the realms of the affective, emotional aspects of learning. In a number of articles and in his book, *Life in Classrooms,* Philip Jackson, Professor of Education and Human Development at the University of Chicago, seems to have picked up where Waller left off in investigating the culture of the school and the sociology of teaching. As chairman of the Association for Supervision and Curriculum Development's Elementary Education Committee in 1969, Jackson was a strong influence in the publication of the booklet, *The Unstudied Curriculum: Its Impact on Children.* This volume of articles includes papers that were presented at an A.S.C.D. conference on the unstudied curriculum in 1969.[13]

Jackson suggests that there are actually two curricula that the young child must learn to master early in the educational experience. One is the traditional or official curriculum of subject matter; learning to read, learning to use numbers, gaining knowledge about the history of our country, about simple science concepts and so on. This is the curriculum for which teachers, administrators, supervisors, and trainers prepare guide books, syllabi, textbooks, workbooks, and, more recently, educational games and programmed learning materials and manuals.

"The other curriculum," Jackson suggests, "Might be described as unofficial or perhaps even hidden, because to date it has received scant attention from educators. The *hidden* curriculum [emphasis, Jackson's] can also be represented by three R's, but not the familiar ones of reading, 'riting, and 'rithmetic. It is, instead, the curriculum of rules, regulations, and routines, of things teachers and students must learn if they are to make their way with minimum pain in the social institution called the school."[14] This second curriculum is possibly the source of difficulty for lower-class or deprived students who are eager to achieve social mobility.

How does Jackson characterize these rules, regulations, and routines? As we describe them, those who work with young children will readily

---

13. *The Unstudied Curriculum: Its Impact on Children*, ed. Norman Overly (Washington, D.C.: Association for Supervision and Curriculum Development, 1970).
14. Philip Jackson, "The Student's World," in *The Experience of Schooling,* ed. Melvin L. Silberman (New York: Holt, Rinehart & Winston, Inc. 1971), p. 20.

recognize these activities. He sees the teacher, especially in the elementary school, as spending a large portion of the time in:

1. *gatekeeping*—managing the flow of traffic in the classroom, deciding who will speak and when, especially during group interactions; who will come and go in and out of the classroom.

2. *allocating resources*—as Jackson adroitly puts it "serving as supply sergeant;" doling out the limited resources in the classroom; granting special privileges to deserving students, assigning coveted duties.

3. *timekeeping*—determining the amount of time for various learning activities; when and who should be dismissed to take the bus; who has been in the lavatory too long, and so on.[15]

Some Comments. If the classroom is organized in the conventional style of the self-contained, teacher-centered tradition, then Jackson's characterizations of gatekeeper, supply sergeant, and timekeeper are accurate but hardly flattering labels for the elementary school teacher. This is particularly appropriate to the early childhood classroom, where it seems an inordinate amount of gatekeeping and timekeeping, as well as adjudicating who can use the material, goes on. "No, John, it is Bill's turn now to have the wagon (or the big truck, or the especially coveted set of wooden cars.)"

If the classroom is organized in what has lately become an increasingly popular movement, in an open-style, informal, British infant school, or small group activities setting, a great deal of the teacher's functioning as gatekeeper, timekeeper and supply sergeant during the ongoing classroom sessions is alleviated. Note the phrase "during the ongoing classroom sessions." Much of the activity in arranging the informal style of the British infant school setting should occur *before* the children enter the room or the school (if the hall and the playgrounds are utilized as well). The teacher performs the functions of a supply sergeant with the additional responsibility of logistician, using careful, advanced planning in the informal, open school. Much of the failure in implementing a type of education in the United States that has proved so successful in England with young children has arisen, this writer feels, because of the lack of recognition of the adroit, astute planning that is required every single day, before and after the children are actually in the classroom.

As one observes open, informal education in America or in England, one quickly notices how the gatekeeper and timekeeper functions so traditional in elementary school classrooms seem to melt away. The children in well-organized open settings go about their business of learn-

---

15. Ibid., pp. 11–13.

ing, studying, small group projects, and so on, with little regard for the clock and with a minimum of traffic jams in the classrooms.

MORE ASPECTS OF THE HIDDEN CURRICULUM

Further, Jackson goes on to point out the frequency of delay, that is, how much of the student's time is spent in waiting. Denial of one's desires, not being able to speak out, to ask questions, thwarting of desire to continue an activity or the denial to participate in it, is yet another aspect of student life. A third quality in classroom settings is that of interruptions—petty misbehaviors, clerical and toileting activities, small distractions so that the students must constantly be "turned back" to their studies. Jackson astutely notes that these three unpublicized features of school life—delay, denial, and interruption, are certainly part of the hidden curriculum.[16]

Some Comments. If one turns to the early childhood classroom organized in the informal open style, many of the petty distractions of delay, denial, and interruptions are minimized. There will always be some type of stress in the interactions of a group of people, but the quality and quantity of these strains can be lessened by the structure and organization of the program in general. In the informal, small group, activity-centers classroom, children are not as apt to be confronted with denials, delays, and interruptions of the projects and activities in which they are engaged.

THE RATING SYSTEM IN THE HIDDEN CURRICULUM

One aspect of school life that is intimately a part of both the official curriculum as well as the hidden curriculum is that of evaluation, testing, and rating. The school child continually takes tests, passes or fails examinations, and is assessed for mastery of cognitive materials, information, and subject matter. The school child is ever involved in informal rating, judging situations with his peers and his teachers. We discussed some of the writings of Waller on this aspect of the culture of the classroom, and Jackson, too, writes with great insight when he describes how teachers of young children are prone to gaze over the class and say things such as "I see that John is a good worker," or "Some people don't seem to know how to follow directions," or *"Lisa has a listening face"* (emphasis added).

A child's peers rate and judge his personality and abilities, but so do his teachers. The cumulative-records school file euphemistically known

---

16. Ibid., pp. 15–16.

in various school districts as "the yellow sheets" or "those G-10 forms" contain comments about pupils: ". . . is a pleasant girl;" ". . . is a hard worker;" ". . . is very aggressive." And then there are the labels applied to children such as "problem child," or "disturbed child." [17]

Some Comments. The rating and judging by teachers and by peers begins early in life, at even three years of age, for the child in the school setting. In the teacher training programs in Great Britain, the new teacher is encouraged to use a form of verbal evaluation that always focuses on the child's actions rather than on his personality. For example, the teacher is trained to say to the young child, "Throwing those blocks might hurt someone," rather than "I don't like boys who throw blocks." Skillful American teachers practice this technique of classroom management, as well, because it minimizes personal judgments of children in negative and detrimental terms that might damage the individual's sense of adequacy. Further, focusing on the child's actions rather than on his personality has a tendency to promote group solidarity, a concern for the welfare of others in the group. This is considered a major emphasis in early childhood education not only in England but even more so in the Soviet Union. This aspect of early training is reiterated again and again in Kitty Weaver's book, *Lenin's Grandchildren: Pre-School Education in the Soviet Union.*

RITUALISM IN PROMOTING GROUP SOLIDARITY

The study of collective behavior, the actions of men in groups, has occupied sociologists and social psychologists since the inception of the discipline. A sociologist who has delved into the intricacies of ritual as it promotes socialization is Orrin Klapp. In his book *Collective Search for Identity*, Klapp delineates a number of aspects or themes in ritual. Klapp defines ritual as "a nondiscursive gestural language, institutionalized for regular occasions, to state sentiments and mystiques that a group values and needs."

> Once seen as language, there is little argument about the general importance of ritual for society, since any language, even one which communicates only vague emotions, helps people to feel more together; and, if emotions are important, then ritual is at least *that* important. So solidarity and fullness of emotional life are two immediate consequences of communicating by ritual. To individuals this means feeling more intensely alive by shared sentiments and mystiques that an individual would not think of by himself.[18]

17. Philip Jackson, *Life in Classrooms* (New York: Holt, Rinehart & Winston, Inc., 1968), p. 23.
18. Orrin Klapp, *Collective Search for Identity.* (New York: Holt, Rinehart & Winston, Inc., 1969), p. 121.

As we investigate the unstudied curriculum, the affective, emotional realms of school life, rituals and ritualism arise as a valid and meaningful aspect of life in classrooms. Klapp's categories or themes of ritualism provide the springboard for applications and examples of the use of rituals in education, and particularly in classrooms of young children.

1. *The ritual of solidarity, fellowship, belongingness.* Belongingness is seen as part of our national character. Americans as a people are "joiners," and regardless of the group, there are varying sorts of ritual which reinforce one's membership in it. Groups have types of uniforms, buttons or pins, special caps, distinct jewelry. One carries a membership card, relates to one's groups in a special location, a clubhouse or meeting place, and so on. Rituals of solidarity and belongingness can be noted in the school setting with the wearing of special types of dress, particularly in parochial schools. Some elementary schools issue a school tee shirt or sweat shirt or school cap. There may be specialized insignias for school books, papers, newsletters or yearbooks that delineate membership in the school group.

One trainer of teachers suggests this technique for teachers of young children: an opening ritual developed by the children which would convey a positive self-image. This could take the form of a series of questions and answers or statements and responses stated alternately by teacher and children:

> *Teacher:* "Today is a great day!"
> *Children:* "Today is the day we have to live."
> *Teacher:* "Today is a great day!"
> *Children:* "We can decide what today will be."

The same trainer of teachers also suggests that mechanical chores such as taking attendance can be carried out in a style that allows the group to feel responsibility for itself by having groups of from four to six students choose one of their number to report absences from that group and announce who will keep track of assignments or messages for those absent.[19]

2. *The ritual of reassurance.* American greeting rituals are an example of this language of reassurance. Eric Berne in *Games People Play* discusses the way Americans greet each other as the giving of "strokes" in which each participant in the conversation reassures the others of their existence.

---

19. Shirley Heckman, "Ritualism—Necessary in Life and in Education," (unpublished paper for Educational Sociology, School of Education, University of Denver, Spring, 1970), p. 14. This author is also grateful to Mrs. Heckman for the suggestions of applications that follow of Orrin Klapp's themes of ritualism to education.

The language of reassurance is expressed in the classroom by greeting each child by name as he or she arrives for the day or in some way recognizing the child's presence in the group that day. Most early childhood programs begin each day with attendance counts or techniques for assessing who is present. But it is the quality of this greeting or recognition which makes it a "stroke," to use Berne's terminology, or makes it a mundane, "so I see you are here" gesture. Teachers of young children are urged to establish practices that are warm, supportive, open and friendly for the traditional "calling the roll" to enhance the child's feeling of pleasure in belonging to his group and to his class.

3. *The rites of status transition.* Anthropologists like to characterize and describe this phenomenon as "rite de passage" in primitive cultures. The literature is replete with examples, some of which are lurid and bizarre. In primitive societies the individual knows clearly when he has arrived at adulthood and what are the privileges and responsibilities that go with such status. In complex, modern, industrialized societies, transition from one age-graded status to the next is blurred and ill-defined. In American society a youth can get a driver's license at 16, must register for the draft at 18, cannot drink beer until he is 21, but can get married any time. And we wonder why there is role confusion in our society.

How are rites of status transition expressed in the early childhood program? If learning to read is recognized as a major achievement and thereby worthy of higher status and honor (as prowess in athletics is so honored at later age levels, especially in the high school), then the teacher can devise techniques for recognition of the three-, four-, or five-year-old who is able to read, or write his name or simple, common words, or add and manipulate numbers. Later, as all the students are reading and writing, recognition can come for completion of various types of readers or storybooks or other types of material. One form this recognition can take is that of allowing the child to pursue his studies independently, rather than with the traditional "reading groups."

4. *The ritual of comic justice, the clown, the fool.* The jesters in medieval courts were the epitome of this role. The court jesters were often physically deformed, dwarfed, or humped-backed. Their diminutive size gave them the privilege of speaking out forthrightly if not embarrassingly about the rulers and royalty of the court, those far above them in social status. The social system conferred immunity on the court jester to criticize and chastise his superiors.

This phenomenon is observed in elementary school classrooms to some degree. Louis Smith and William Geoffrey in their book *The Complexities of An Urban Classroom*, describe two variations of this role taken by elementary school pupils. The *Clown* "a role in which a pupil provokes humor, usually at his own expense." The *Court Jester* "a classroom role in which a pupil engages in humorous, taunting teasing of the teacher (often but not necessarily the class clown)." [20]

The teacher often handles the class clown or the "court jester" in the classroom setting by simply ignoring the troublesome child. But the child taking these roles may not desist from his behavior and will manage to distract others from an ongoing activity. One thoughtful teacher found a creative way of handling the court jester in the class by allowing him a short time at the end of the day to "put on his act" in front of the class, his audience, while she stepped aside and joined the class. In this case, the technique was most effective. The child turned to positive outlets of expression rather than sarcastic mimicry, while the rest of the class listened and enjoyed his performance.

5. *The ritual of reciprocity.* The giving of gifts and of greeting cards to those who send them to you are illustrations of this kind of ritual. This reciprocity of gift or token giving is obvious in the Valentine Day "ceremonies" in classrooms of young children, when children exchange valentines.

Early childhood teachers often like to have their children decorate paper bags or shoe boxes several days before the Valentine's Day party. This gives the children an opportunity to do a creative art project and also to write their name on the box or bag. The children are then directed to bring enough valentine cards for each person in the class. On the appointed day the children distribute their valentines, dropping one in each box. Sometimes a teacher will suggest that each child write his own name on the valentine, saying "from _____." Again this gives the child practice in writing his own name with a reasonable purpose in mind rather than just monotonous repetition of a group of letters. Sometimes four or five-year-olds like to count the valentines they receive as an indication of their popularity with their peers. The teacher of young children who senses this tendency among her students can organize valentine card exchanges as described above so that all the children get approximately the same number of cards, hence a ritual of reciprocity.

6. *The ritual of kinship extension*: once again the anthropological literature contains ethnographic data detailing the intricacies, ceremonies, and rituals surrounding exchanges between families when a wedding is to occur. A marriage in simpler societies entails the establishment of an alliance between families or clans with mutual obligations and responsibilities when the groups are united. In contemporary society this phenomenon can be seen when such customs as those of some blacks on the west

---

20. Louis Smith and William Geoffrey, *The Complexities of An Urban Classroom.* (New York: Holt, Rinehart & Winston, Inc., 1968), p. 264.

side of Chicago greet each other with the salutation of "bro-in-law" and "sist-in-law," the syllables all run together. The sense of kinship and bonds of mutuality are thus verbalized by those wishing to establish a broader kinship.

In classrooms of young children, the ritual of kinship extension is observed in the way new class members are received by those already established in the class. With young children these ceremonies or customs of welcoming a new arrival to the group, are often initiated and planned by the teacher. In one class where many new students arrived about every other week, the children themselves set up and carried through welcoming procedures. They assigned a child to be a "buddy" for the new class member, helping him to check out books, explaining classroom procedures and rules, and locating facilities for him in the school building. A related process was developed for those who were moving out of the classroom. These procedures involved the celebration of their having been part of the group and the indication to the children leaving of their importance as persons in that group. This class established a rapport and esprit de corps that was unusual to find even among adult groups and organizations.

7. *The rituals of oaths and resolutions which bind a person to a path or obligation.* The formalized ritual of the wedding ceremony with its marriage vows is an example of this type of ritual. Legal contracts and documents also bind the individual to prescribed duties and obligations. The sworn oath to uphold the laws of the land when taking public office exemplifies the verbal expression of an oath.

Young children are seldom called upon to sign "legal" contracts or swear oaths of allegiance with deeply serious intent where serious consequences would follow if the bonds are broken. Yet the practice of signing contracts obligating the child to take on a specified amount of study and work has arisen recently with the technique of teaching through "performance contracting." This custom is part of the program in open style, individualized classroom settings where each child establishes with his teacher, and his parents as well, how much he is going to cover during a specified amount of time. The child signs a "contract" agreeing to cover so much reading, so much arithmetic, and so on. At the assigned date, his performance is evaluated by the teacher and the results are given to the child to bring home for his parents to see.

In the area of the verbalized oath or swearing of allegiance, the mental picture of a group of children, hands on their hearts, saying the oath of allegiance to the flag as they face the front of the room where a flag is usually displayed comes to mind. Some humorous stories have been told about how young children mispronounce or misunderstand the unfamiliar words in the "Pledge of Allegiance" or in songs such as "The Star

Spangled Banner." One such example is told of the child who when illustrating the song "America, The Beautiful" portrayed the line "Oh, beautiful for fruited plains" with a drawing of airplanes, their wings covered with apples, oranges, and bananas — the "fruited planes"! This has led some teachers of young children to develop and use simplified versions of the "Pledge of Allegiance," such as the following "fingerplay":

The thoughts of my head (hands on head),
The work of my hands (place hands palms up),
The love of my heart (place right hand on heart),
I give to you my flag (place hands palms up again).

8. *The ritual of pomp and ceremony.* Formal resolutions and the public announcement of bonds of obligation usually take place at ceremonies. Weddings are ceremonies, the celebration of holidays with parades and pageants are forms of ceremonies. In former days the crowning of rulers, coronations, religious festivals were all rituals of pomp and ceremony that served to develop group solidarity and create bonds and ties among people.

In the school setting the most obvious example of the ritual of pomp and ceremony is that of graduation. In schools for young children the practice of graduation has sometimes been used in quite ludicrous ways by having a "kindergarten" graduation ceremony. When an individual is just beginning his career as a student, which certainly characterizes five-year-olds in school, to have him perform in a ritual that was designed for signifying the termination of one's studies seems deceiving and inappropriate. Yet those working in programs for young children should not overlook the power and mystique that is generated by school assemblies, programs in the "auditorium" or the all-purpose room that bring together several classes of children. In the British primary schools an assembly is held every morning attended by all the children in the school. This gives the head mistress or head master (the principal) the opportunity to lead in a ceremony that develops deep ties and feelings of mutuality among all those who participate, children and teachers alike.

Further, the celebration of holidays throughout the school year, especially Halloween, creates occasions for ceremonies, such as dressing up in funny costumes and parading about the school, that function to bring group solidarity and the feeling of belongingness to a special group of people.

9. *The ritual of moral affirmation.* The bringing of the criminal, the perpetrator of crimes against the people, to justice through trial and public knowledge of the crimes committed can be described as moral affirmation. Literature contains materials such as morality plays, "crime doesn't pay"-type dramas, stories of one's moral debt to society and the punishment of those who do not fulfill their obligations.

Emile Durkheim in the *Elementary Forms of Religious Life,* at the turn of the century wrote extensively on morality and its implication for education in complex societies. Durkheim's theories as well as others have been utilized by Lawrence Kohlberg of Harvard University to study morality, values, and morals among children in elementary schools in the United States and in various countries around the globe. This work on the moral atmosphere of the school is so central to the theme of this book that we will devote the next pages to discussing and describing the research and writings of Kohlberg on what he eloquently terms "investigating the child as a moral philosopher."

INVESTIGATING MORAL CLIMATE IN THE CLASSROOM

In studies that view the young child's classroom as a social arena, a central theme is that social life in the classroom is a microcosm of social life in the broader society, the macrocosm. The school is characterized as the institution of society that prepares the young to function in the adult world. This is the "mother culture," the "idee maitresse," upon which is built the rituals, ceremonies, customs, folkways, traditions that form the hidden, unstudied curriculum. Schooling has been described as an intensive experience in institutional living. The whole array of rules and regulations are sanctioned by that higher authority, the common good. We do it for the safety and well being of the group. This is how teachers of young children reply to the questions of "Why do we. . . ?" Now when we construe the essence of rules and regulations in the school setting to a higher order, a greater good than the individual's purposes, we place the locus of authority in dimensions of morality. With this reasoning then, Lawrence Kohlberg states that the only integrated way of thinking about the hidden curriculum is to think of it as moral education.[21]

Kohlberg turns to the work of Emile Durkheim to support his proposition that life in classrooms is actually learning to live in a group where there is impersonal authority (as opposed to one's home, where there are familial ties). Durkheim wrote that the school environment is the most desirable for preparing the child to live in the adult world because the school is an institution that results from neither blood-ties nor from free choice, but is created by the society to bring individuals of similar age and condition together. Durkheim was the first social scientist to theorize that the workings of society are actually a form of morality—rational and scientific morality. He points out that the acceptance of authority is one of the key elements of the child's moral development.

---

21. Lawrence Kohlberg, "The Moral Atmosphere of the School," in *The Unstudied Curriculum: Its Impact on Children,* edited by Norman Overly (Association of Supervision and Curriculum Development, 1970), p. 104.

Morality is respect for rule and is altruistic attachment to the social group. . . . although family education is an excellent preparation for the moral life, its usefulness is restricted, above all with respect to the spirit of discipline. That which is essential to the spirit of discipline, respect for the rule, can scarcely develop in the familial setting, which is not subject to general impersonal immutable regulaton, and should have an air of freedom. But the child must learn respect for the rule; he must learn to do his duty because it is his duty, even though the task may not seem an easy one. . . .

School discipline is not a simple device for securing superficial peace in the classroom; *it is the morality of the classroom as a small society* (emphasis added).[22]

Kohlberg derives his thesis that the hidden curriculum is actually moral education from the theory laid down by Durkheim. The child is socialized and enculturated in his classroom into the morality of his society.

DURKHEIM'S CONCEPTS OF EDUCATION AS SOCIAL CONTROL

In his book *The Division of Labor in Society,* Durkheim describes two differing types of social order. One type has highly specialized roles, diverse jobs, where a loss of a particular group of specialists might impair the whole society. Here the individuals in the society have *achieved* their roles and their status in the group, and there is a complex interdependence of specialized functions. This type of social integration Durkheim labels "organic solidarity." On the other hand, a society that possesses "mechanical solidarity" is characterized by ascribed roles. Here the society could prevail even if a large portion of its members were removed. When a society possesses mechanical solidarity the individuals will share a common system of belief with detailed regulations on conduct and morality. When rules and regulations are broken, punishment is necessary in order to keep the common system of beliefs intact and inviolable.

When the society is highly complex and specialized, and social organization manifests organic solidarity, the aim is less to punish infractions than it is to reconcile conflicting claims. Social control is seen as restitutive and reparative rather than repressive. Our nation is certainly a highly complex society manifesting organic solidarity in Durkheimian terms. Punishment for breaking the rules or the laws is first of all cast in terms of restoring the individual to the society, rather than casting him out of the group altogether. In the school setting we appeal in the initial reaction less to the aspect that a "sacred" dictum has been broken, than to *who* did it and *why*.

If this technique for social control is true of American schools, it also

---

22. Emile Durkheim, *Moral Education* (New York: The Free Press, Inc., 1961 [Originally published posthumously in 1925]), p. 148.

А Аа Аа Аа Аа

Лена поймала ёжи

ка. Мм Пп Нн Тт

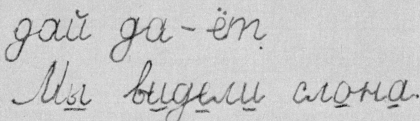

пей поёт

дай да-ёт.

Мы видели слона.

Нн Лл Аа

я я я я я я я я я я я я

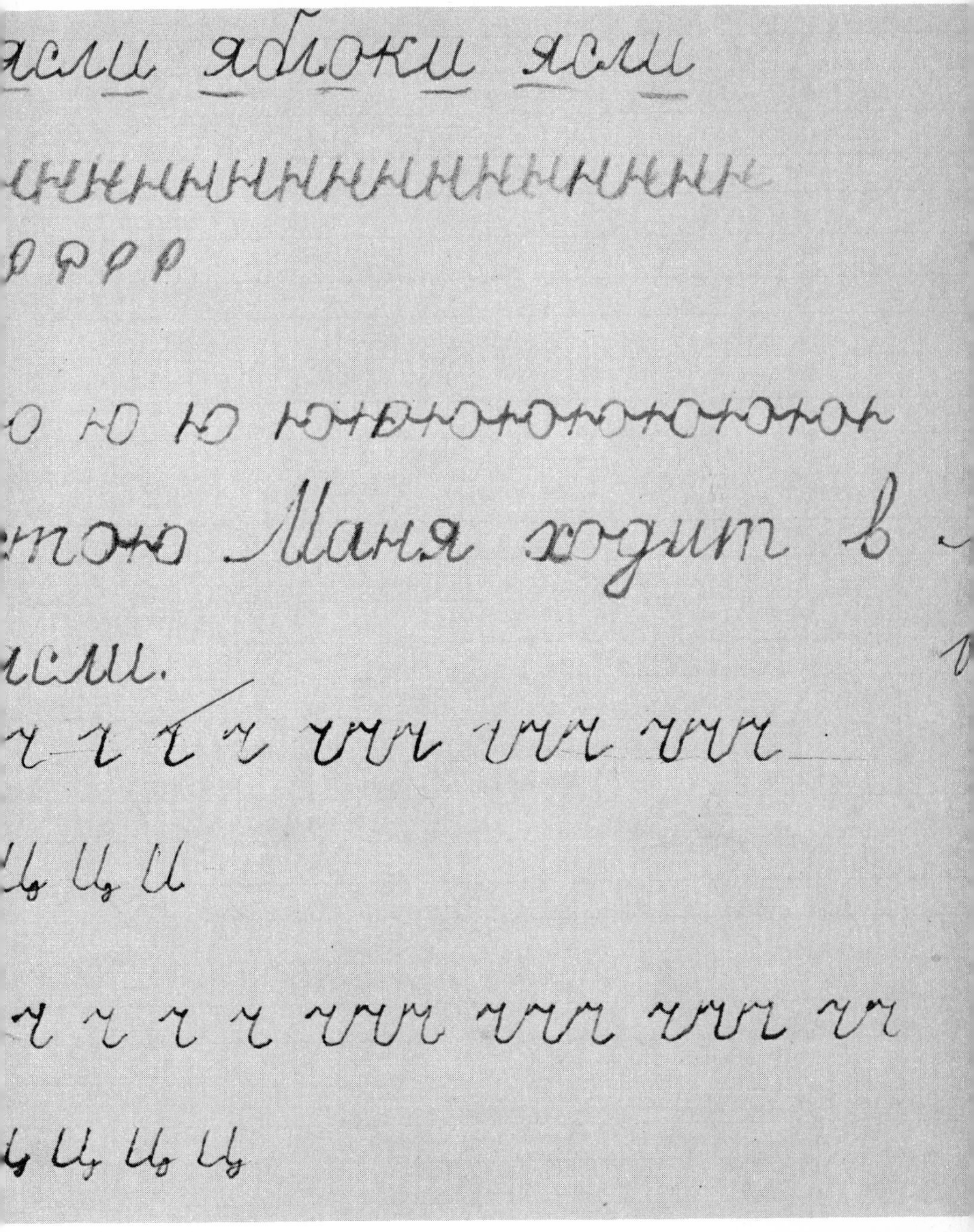

ясли яблоки ясли

ннннннннннннннн

р р р р

ю ю ю юнюнюнюнюнюнюнюн

тою Маня ходит в

ясли.
ч ч ч ч чч чч чч

ц ц ц

ч ч ч ч чч чч чч чч

ц ц ц ц

Fig. 1.2. Soviet child's practice writing book. (Courtesy Eleanor Pennington, Westminster, Colorado Public Schools.)

characterizes British education today. Basil Bernstein, educational sociologist at the University of London, writes:

> In [British] schools there has been a move away from the transmission of common values through a ritual order and control based upon position or status, to more personalized forms of control where teachers and taught confront each other as individuals. The forms of social control appeal less to shared values, group loyalties and involvements; they are based rather upon the recognition of differences between individuals. With this change there has been a weakening of the symbolic significance and ritualization of punishment.[23]

Yet we noted earlier in this chapter that teachers of young children in both the United States and in England are being trained to discipline children by appealing to the needs of the group, cooperating for the common good. The fact is that both techniques of social control are utilized in the schools of the United States and Britain. In complex nations characterized by organic solidarity, social control in the educational setting is exercised by appealing to loyalty for the group and by personalized forms of control. Now turning to the literature on education in the Soviet Union, and particularly the writings on early childhood education, we find that the stress is on the collective good, altruistic actions, the greater welfare of the group. This comes across clearly in Kitty Weaver's account of Russian pre-schools mentioned earlier, and in Urie Bronfenbrenner's outstanding book on Soviet early childhood education, *Two Worlds of Childhood: U.S. and U.S.S.R.*

THE HIDDEN CURRICULUM AS MORE THAN SOCIAL CONTROL

It would seem that schools for young children have a greater purpose than to introduce the rudiments of the academic curriculum and prepare the child for life in a complex, industrialized society. Kohlberg poses this question insightfully when he asks if moral education has some other aims than establishing a loyalty to the school and to other children which might possibly later transfer to loyalty to the nation and to other men. He suggests that the intellectual, cognitive aspects of the curriculum need not be irreconcilably divorced from the affective, emotional, social areas of the curriculum.

> The assumption is that the child is controlled by primitive and selfish drives he is reluctant to give up and that the steady experience of authority and discipline is necessary to live with rules. The notions of Dewey and Piaget, that the child genuinely learns to accept authority when he learns to understand and accept the reasons and principles behind

23. Basil Bernstein, "Open Schools, Open Society," *Education: A New Society Social Studies Reader* (London: New Society, 1971), p. 12.

the rules, leads moral education in a different direction, tied much more closely to the intellectual curriculum of the school. This second direction is supported by many research findings. My research and that of others indicates that the development of moral character is in large part a sequential progressive growth of basic principles of moral reasoning and their application to action.[24]

We have already briefly presented the Piagetian stages of mental growth: the sensori-motor stage, the pre-operational stage, the stage of concrete operations, and the stage of formal operations. Piaget feels that one cannot really separate the cognitive intellectual components of behavior from those components that function in the affective domain. "The two aspects, affective and cognitive, are at the same time inseparable and irreducible. It is precisely this unity of behavior which makes the factors in development common to both the cognitive and the affective aspects."[25]

Hence as the individual progresses through the stages of mental development, his behavior manifest patterns that are both cognitive and affective, according to Piaget. It is upon this premise that Kohlberg has postulated distinct stages in the moral development of the individual grounded in Piagetian theory. Kohlberg begins his formulation, however, with the pre-operational stage in the child's thinking at about the age of six or seven. Through the use of stories and recounts of situations, Kohlberg and his associates have posed moral dilemmas and public policy dilemmas to children in elementary and secondary schools throughout the world. Children in Mexico, Great Britain, Taiwan, Turkey, the United States, and Canada have participated in these studies of moral development for over a decade. The six stages of moral development, according to Kohlberg, are cast into three levels. These levels are:

1. *The pre-conventional level.* Here the child is responsive to cultural rules and labels of good and bad, right or wrong. One is punished or rewarded for his actions, and physical power determines who metes out these responses.

Within the first level of moral development are stages 1 and 2. *Stage 1* is a punishment and obedience orientation; here one tries to avoid punishment but unquestioningly bows to power. *Stage 2* is a right action satisfying one's own need orientation.

2. *The conventional level.* Here conformity of one's personal desires to the social order, the group's needs, comes first, regardless of the cost to the individual.

Within the second level of moral development are stages 3 and 4. *Stage 3* is labeled the "good boy—good girl" orientation where one earns ap-

---

24. Kohlberg, "The Moral Atmosphere of the School," p. 115.
25. Jean Piaget and Barbel Inhelder, *The Psychology of the Child* (New York: Basic Books, 1969), p. 158.

proval by being "nice." While *Stage 4* is the "law and order" orientation, right behavior consists of doing one's duty and showing respect for authority.

3. *The post-conventional level.* This is the clear effort to define moral principles and values on a universal scale for all humankind.

Within the third level of moral development are stages 5 and 6. *Stage 5* takes a social-contract, legalistic orientation. Finally, at *Stage 6* one reaches the mature posture of the universal ethical principle orientation.

It is obvious that young children under eight years of age cannot be functioning at the post-conventional level of moral development, since stages 5 and 6 or Kohlberg's categories are based on advanced reasoning, logic, and the ability to use language and symbolism. Kohlberg states that a series of carefully replicated experimental studies have demonstrated that children seldom comprehend messages of moral judgments more than one stage above their own level, and understand but reject messages below their own level of moral comprehension. He goes on to note that with young children it is clear that we can make the mistake of both being on too high or on too low a level. Moreover, it is worse to make the mistake of being at too low a level because the child loses respect for the message being presented.[26]

AN APPLICATION OF KOHLBERG'S STAGES TO YOUNGER CHILDREN

Kohlberg used stories that posed moral dilemmas in assessing the stages of moral development in the children he studied. These stories and anecdotes appear too sophisticated and complex to pose to children under ten years of age. This writer and several graduate students developed some stories and materials to present to children ages six to nine years old and attempted to replicate informally some of Kohlberg's studies with younger children. A sample of 30 white, middle-class, six-, seven-, and eight-year-olds was presented the following stories in an individual interview situation where the investigator interacted with one child at a time, posing the moral dilemma and asking each child to respond. The interviews were carried on in a public school, in a quiet area adjoining the classroom. Care was taken to use a neutral tone of voice and limited facial expression so that the child would respond with his own opinions and not be influenced by the reactions of the interviewer to his remarks.

Here are the moral dilemma stories that we developed for six, seven and eight year olds:

------

26. Kohlberg, "The Moral Atmosphere of the School," pp. 118–19.

The Birthday Parties

There was a little boy named Joe, just about your age who had parents whose birthdays were on the very same day. There was to be a party for both of them and, of course, Joe was invited to go. But then he was also invited to go to another party for his best friend.

What would you do if you had to choose between your parents' birthday party and a birthday party for your very best friend? Why?

Now Joe had only enough money to buy one present. He knew his big sister had some money in her purse, but he couldn't find her to ask her if he could have some to buy a present. Someone was ready right away to take him shopping for the presents, so Joe took some money from his sister's purse anyway.

Should he have done that? Was it all right or was it wrong? Why?

Joe's sister discovered that her money was gone and when Joe returned from shopping she asked him if he thought Sally, the other sister, had taken the money from the purse. Joe replied that he had seen Sally in her room looking around in the purse.

Should Joe have said that about Sally? Why?

Should Joe have told his sister that he took the money from her purse? Why?

You will note that this story about birthday parties presents three moral dilemmas. This was purposefully done to take into account the shorter attention span of younger children and the need to set before them one problem at a time for their consideration.

A Mouse

A little boy was playing and found a little mouse trapped in a window well. He picked it up and held it very tightly. Then he played with the mouse some more. He soon discovered the mouse wouldn't move any more and that it was dead.

How do you think the little boy felt?

The teacher who composed these stories of moral dilemmas noted that once she had observed a three-year-old who had discovered a small mouse, played with it a while, and actually squeezed it to death. The child said he thought the mouse just had a broken leg that was why it lay so still. His lack of compassion for the mouse and his crushing it by holding it too tightly made this teacher wonder if, by the age of six, children began to show compassion for small animals. As an interviewer in this study, she noted that the children involved responded to the story of the mouse with little verbalization, but with expressions on their face that indicated a feeling of sadness over the death of the mouse. She writes,

Perhaps the most significant point in their answers was that only two children, the older "eights" recognized that the mouse, was dead because the boy had killed him. They could see the consequences of the boy's actions, whereas the others could only recognize the results and not the connection. Piaget pointed out that a child must progress in his stages of intellectual and moral development to a certain point before he can see another's point of view or put himself in the place of the other.[27]

RESULTS FROM THE CHILDREN

How did the children respond to these stories? Were they able to answer the questions? How would their answers be categorized according to Kohlberg's stages?

Since the stories presented realistic and familiar situations to the children, they were able to respond.

Dilemma 1: Choosing between your own parents' birthday party and your best friend's party. Of 30 children asked, 17 chose the parents' party, nine chose the best friend's party, three said they would go to neither party, and one child said he would try to make both of the parties. The 56 percent majority of the children who chose the parents' birthday party gave reasons such as "They are my parents," or "They are more important." Those who chose the friend's party over the parents' party (30 per cent) gave reasons such as "I could play more," or "I could make a dummy to go to Mom and Dad's party and I would go to the friend's party myself." These responses would put the children at stages 1 and 2 or the preconventional level of moral thinking. The responses stem from bowing to the more powerful force (one's parents) or from an irrational, "it is because it is" basis. One child is totally unrealistic in his response, knowing that a "dummy" would easily be discovered by his parents, but uses this reasoning anyway.

None of the children advanced the reason that one would attend his parents' party because his family expected it of him and it was his duty to his family group—a stage 3 or 4 type response.

Dilemma 2: Should Joe have taken the money from his sister's purse without telling her, even though he had to go shopping right away and couldn't find her? Twenty-seven of the thirty children responded that Joe should not have taken the money from his sister's purse, and only three children responded that it would be all right to do so. Yet the children's reasons, such as "You shouldn't take money" or "It would be stealing" were indicative of the pre-conventional level of thinking.

---

27. Bernice Wallace, "Applications of Kohlberg's Theory of Moral Development in the Child" (unpublished paper for Human Growth and Development, School of Education, University of Denver, December, 1970), p. 9.

Dilemma 3: Should Joe have told his sister a false story implicating his older sister, Sally? And should Joe have told his sister the truth that he took the money from her purse?

To both questions, all the children, unanimously, indicated that Joe was wrong to have implicated his sister and was wrong in not telling the truth about his actions. By six years of age children have begun to develop a sense of morality, and they reason that lying and stealing are wrong things to do. Yet the responses to "why" indicate that most of the group were at the pre-conventional level of moral reasoning. Their replies, such as "It was lying," "It was wrong," or "He would get into trouble" do not indicate concern for the common good, or concern about others' feelings. Two children, eight-year-olds, did give these reasons for why it was wrong that Joe falsely indicated it might be Sally's fault that the money was missing: "It would hurt Sally's feelings" and "Sally would get Joe's spanking." These children were giving indications that they did recognize the feelings of others, a tendency at the conventional level of thinking.

The responses to the story of the mouse have already been briefly reviewed, but of the 30 children in the sample responding to the question of how the little boy felt when he found the mouse was dead, 28 of them replied with "sad," "bad," or "sorry." Only two children replied that the boy felt "good" about the mouse's death. The two older children who indicated they realized the consequences of the boy's actions in squeezing the mouse, stated: "He killed it while playing around with it," and "He'd killed something he'd tried to save and couldn't," while most of the children replied simply, "It was dead" or "It died."

Our analysis of the responses of the children and the categorizing of the children's remarks into stages according to Kohlberg's theories, must be viewed as a tentative, informal and experimental approach to using Kohlberg's material with children under ten years of age. Kohlberg has developed detailed analysis systems for categorizing the responses obtained from children in the samples he and his associates have studied. The experimental study here is presented as an example of what could be developed for younger children. Our work applying stages of moral development to the thinking of young children is also presented to illustrate Kohlberg's ideas and theories on moral development as an aspect of intellectual development based in Piagetian theory, since Piaget writes that the child in the pre-operational stage will evaluate a lie "to be serious not to the degree that it corresponds to the intent to deceive, but to the degree that it differs from the objective truth."[28]

As we stated, most of the children indicated the reason the acts of lying and stealing were wrong would fall in the category of "not the objective

---

28. Jean Piaget and Barbel Inhelder. *The Psychology of the Child,* p. 126.

truth" rather than "intent to deceive." The study of children's moral judgments at the pre-operational level of the six- to eight-year-olds provides
us with examples of how the cognitive and the affective aspects intertwine.

WHITHER THE HIDDEN CURRICULUM AND
MORAL EDUCATION?

So Kohlberg has presented us with a new perspective of the hidden
curriculum. It is a curriculum of moral education that contains both the
intellectual, cognitive domain and the emotive, affective domain in its content. From research studies that have used discussions of social policy and
moral dilemmas in secondary school classes, a viable curriculum in moral
education has been proven to be feasible. Such a curriculum, Kohlberg
feels, should not exist in abstraction, however; it should exist as a reflection
of the hidden curriculum of school life.

> The hidden curriculum of the school must represent something more
> than the goals and social order of the school itself. Our definition of
> moral maturity as the principled sense of justice suggest what this end
> must be. The teaching of justice requires just schools. . . . In our
> society authority derives from justice, and in our society learning to
> live with authority should derive from and aid learning to understand
> and to feel justice.
> The need to make the hidden curriculum an atmosphere of justice,
> and to make this hidden curriculum explicit in intellectual and verbal
> discussions of justice and morality, is becoming more and more urgent.[29]

Here then, we have a conception of life in American classrooms as
training and preparation for children to live in a society where social justice
and universal human rights provide the morality for law and order.

DID WE MAKE THE SCENE?

Where has our investigation into the social arena that is the classroom
of young children led us? Some sensitive and aware social scientists have
been writing about the child's social world for decades. But it has just been
in recent years that educators have deeply concerned themselves with the
hidden, unstudied curriculum. This aspect of school life has been called
by a variety of labels and titles. Waller titles it the culture of the school;
Jackson prefers life in classrooms or the hidden curriculum; Melvin Silberman labels it the experience of schooling; the anthropological approach
is called the microethnology of the classroom; and Durkheim and Kohlberg
see the social life in schools as the moral atmosphere in the classroom and
the curriculum in moral education. Life in classrooms begins for the child

---

29. Kohlberg, "The Moral Atmosphere of the School," pp. 121–22.

Fig. 1.3. "My dog and I call for help on the phone"—seven-year-old, Denver, Colorado.

on the day he enters school, when he is three or four or five years of age. Teachers of young children should be particularly aware of the impact of the hidden curriculum because its effects are pivotal and irreversible in the lives of very young children. Bloom and his associates have provided us with research that indicates the typical individual attains about 50 percent of his ultimate intellectual ability by the age of four, and another 30 percent increase in intellectual ability between the ages of four and eight. Just as the studies of intellectual development have shown that the crucial years in human intellectual development are the first eight years of life, so too, could we state that these are the crucial years in emotional development.

In the next chapter we will present the theories of sociologist, Erving Goffman on one's presentation of self, social interaction in the context of a stage where the individual is characterized as presenting a performance for his audience. This performance may become blemished by stigmas which create a "spoiled identity" for the individual.

Sources

Berne, Eric. *Games People Play*. New York: Grove Press, 1968.

Bloom, Benjamin. *Stability and Change in Human Characteristics*. New York: John Wiley & Sons, 1964.

Bronfenbrenner, Urie. *Two Worlds of Childhood: U.S. and U.S.S.R.* New York: Russell Sage Foundation, 1970.

Dreeben, Robert. *On What Is Learned in School*. Reading, Mass.: Addison, Wesley Publishing Co., 1968.

Durkheim, Emile. *The Division of Labor in Society*. New York: Free Press, 1947.

——————————. *Elementary Forms of Religious Life*. New York: Free Press, 1954.

——————————. *Moral Education*. New York: Free Press, 1961.

Jackson, Philip. *Life in Classrooms*. New York: Holt, Rinehart & Winston, Inc., 1968.

Klapp, Orrin. *Collective Search for Identity*. New York: Holt, Rinehart & Winston, Inc., 1969.

Kohlberg, Lawrence. "The Child as a Moral Philosopher," *Psychology Today* (1968), pp. 241-31.

Lavatelli, Celia S. *A Piagetian Approach to an Early Childhood Curriculum*. Boston: American Science and Engineering, 1971.

Maccoby, Eleanor. "The Development of Moral Values and Behavior in Childhood." In *Socialization and Society* edited by J. Clausen, pp. 227-269. New York: Little Brown, 1968.

Overly, Norman, ed. *The Unstudied Curriculum: Its Impact on Children*. Washington: Association of Supervision and Curriculum Development, 1970.

Piaget, Jean. *The Moral Judgment of the Child*. New York: Free Press of Glencoe, 1948.

——————— and Inhelder, Barbel, *The Psychology of the Child.* New York: Basic Books, 1969.

Silberman, Melvin, ed. *The Experience of Schooling.* New York: Holt, Rinehart & Winston, Inc., 1971.

Smith, Louis and Geoffrey, William. *The Complexities of an Urban Classroom.* New York: Holt, Rinehart & Winston, Inc., 1968.

Waller, Willard. *The Sociology of Teaching.* New York: John Wiley & Sons, Inc., 1965.

Weaver, Kitty. *Lenin's Grandchildren: Pre-School Education in the Soviet Union.* New York: Simon and Schuster, 1971.

chapter 2

Stigma and the Young Child

The analogy of life as a stage with individuals playing out their roles as actors in a setting is an old one dating back to Shakespeare and perhaps even before his immortal rhetoric that all the world's a stage and all the people merely players upon it. Occasionally in the literature, teachers have been referred to as actors, playing out their dramas in the classroom. Life in classrooms has been the topic and the theme of numerous films, novels, and plays. Some teachers, particularly in high schools and in higher education, develop a reputation for dramatic histrionics in the classroom, as though they were truly "on stage" giving a performance. Some of these very teachers are considered the most outstanding and dedicated by their students and their colleagues. A highly dramatic and theatrical technique in the appropriate context in teaching can be a vehicle to optimum learning rather than a distracting condition. Sometimes teachers of young children employ a theatrical stance when telling or reading stories to the children. The whole tradition and art of the storyteller has been an intimate sector of early childhood education since the founding of the kindergarten.

Rare in the literature on teaching methodology and practice, however, is an examination of the mundane, day-to-day experience of teachers and students in the framework or the metaphor of theatrical performance. As we have been describing the hidden curriculum, the experience that attending school becomes for children and teachers alike, it is apparent that a framework of a body of concepts and theories would be immensely helpful for categorizing and analyzing just what *is* going on between individuals. It is at this point, then, that this writer turns to the work and the theories of sociologist Erving Goffman as a meaningful and extremely pertinent model for examining life in classrooms. Goffman's theories were originally developed to view men and women in everyday social intercourse. Goff-

Fig. 2.1. "This is the way I think I look because people can't understand me" —kindergartner, Westwood School, Denver, Colorado. (Courtesy Beverly Gonzalez, kindergarten teacher.)

man has employed the theatrical metaphor or the dramaturgic approach in sociology to examining people as they present themselves and their activities to others and try to guide and control the impression they create. The sociologist sees the individual employing certain techniques in order to sustain his performance, just as the actor presents a character to an audience. This dramaturgic sociology has been built upon detailed and painstaking research and observation of social customs in many regions of the United States and in Europe.

"In Goffman's theory the conventional cultural hierarchies are shattered: for example, professional psychiatrists are manipulated by hospital inmates; doubt is cast upon the difference between the cynical and the sincere; the behavior of children becomes a model for understanding adults; the behavior of criminals becomes a standpoint for understanding respectable people; the theater's stage becomes a model for understanding life," writes Alvin Gouldner in *The Coming Crisis in Western Sociology.*[1] Gouldner goes on to note that Goffman's dramaturgic sociology advances a view in which social life is systematically regarded as an elaborate form of drama as in the theatre where men are continually striving to project a convincing image of themselves to others.

APPLYING GOFFMAN'S THEORIES TO EARLY CHILDHOOD CLASSROOMS

In order to apply Goffman's theories to the everyday life of teachers and students in early childhood classrooms, it seems necessary to delineate the terminology and concepts that the sociologist has developed to examine groups of people and their social customs. The following definitions of terms and concepts as used by Goffman have been taken from *The Presentation of Self in Everyday Life,* one of the earliest and seminal writings of the sociologist.[2]

Performance—"refers to all the activity of an individual which occurs during a period marked by his continuous presence before a particular set of observers and which has some influence on the observers" (p. 22).

Front—"that part of the individual's performance which regularly functions in a general and fixed fashion to define the situation for those who observe the performance. It is the expressive equipment of a standard kind intentionally or unwittingly employed by the individual during his performance" (p. 22).

Setting—" a standard part of *front* involving furniture, decor, physical layout, and other background items which supply the scenery and stage props for the human action played out before, within, or upon it" (p. 22).

Personal Front—"refers to the other items of expressive equipment, the items that we most intimately identify with the performer himself; his insignia of office or rank; clothing; sex; age; racial characteristics; size and looks; posture; speech patterns; facial expressions; bodily gestures; and the like" (p. 24).

Dramatic Realization—"the individual typically infuses his performance with signs which dramatically highlight and portray confirmatory facts

---

1. Alvin W. Gouldner. *The Coming Crisis in Western Sociology.* (New York: Basic Books, 1970), p. 379.
2. Erving Goffman, *Presentation of Self in Everyday Life* (Garden City: Doubleday & Co., Inc.), 1959.

that might otherwise remain unapparent or obscure. For if the individual's activity is to become significant to others, he must mobilize his activity so that it will express *during the interaction* what he wishes to convey" (p. 30).

Idealization—"describes a performance that is 'socialized,' molded and modified to fit into the understanding and expectations of the society in which it is presented. . . . Thus when the individual presents himself before others his performance will tend to incorporate and exemplify the officially accredited values of the society, more so, in fact, than does his behavior as a whole" (p. 35).

Mystification—is the "maintenance of social distance that provides a way in which we can be generated and sustained in the audience" (p. 67).

Audience—the observers who view the performance.

How then can we apply Goffman's model to teachers and students, and more specifically to education in the early childhood setting? We begin with the *performance*. The teacher is providing a performance in the class room when he or she is engaged in an activity—teaching—during a period of time—the school day (in early childhood programs this can be a half day session or an all-day session). Further, the teacher is in the continued presence of a set of observers—the students—and is influencing their behavior.

The performer, the teacher, constructs a *front* which incorporates a *personal front* and is enacted within a *setting*. The setting in which the teacher plays out the performance is a classroom whose decor or physical layout includes walls, bulletin and chalk boards, furniture—the teacher's desk, the smaller, child-sized tables and chairs; the bookshelves, cupboards, and closets stocked with materials; the doll corner or play house; the games area, science corner, etc. These elements have been carefully arranged by the teacher. The teacher's personal front consists of far more maturity in age, greater size and strength, greater wisdom and experience than the young students before whom the performance takes place. The teacher's personal front might also include the dress, mannerisms, style of speech and expressions that have been cultivated for this performance, the instruction of young children.

Goffman turns to the medical profession to give an example of the arbitrary nature of the setting for the performance. He notes that it is increasingly important for a doctor to have access to the elaborate scientific stage provided by large hospitals, so that fewer and fewer doctors are able to feel that their setting is a place that they can lock up at night.[3]

Much the same comments could be made about the elaborate setting of modern early childhood education programs with the ever-growing range of educational toys, games, curriculum materials, Montessori and Piagetian

---

3. Ibid., p. 23.

materials, blocks, water toys, building tools, manipulative equipment, large and small muscle toys, as well as picture books, workbooks, alphabet cards, art materials, rhythm instruments, physical education apparatus. In order for the teacher of young children to adequately perform in the setting, some educators today are advocating such an elaborate set of scenery and props that the impact of the teacher's personal front, style, personal charm, warmth, knowledge, and ability in working with youngsters, are all but forgotten.

When we think of teachers of young children we invariably picture a *woman*—youngish or older, with a sweet smile and a gentle demeanor. Goffman points out that a given social front tends to become stereotyped and institutionalized. This expectation of front, social or personal, of the teacher of young children is certainly characteristic of U.S. society. Now recently when men, usually innovative, dynamic, creative, open-minded young men, choose to become teachers for groups of children under eight years of age, they must establish a personal front that is part of a new performance in the society, while also counteracting a long-standing stereotypical role, the old-maidish kindergarten teacher.

We have used Goffman's concepts of the performance, front, setting, and personal front in application to teachers of young children. Now let us see how his terms *dramatic realization, idealization,* and *mystification* fit into life in classrooms. *Dramatic realization* has been outlined as a technique which the performer uses to infuse his performance with dramatic highlights, emphasizing what might otherwise remain obscure. He has to underscore his activity to impress upon his observers or audience aspects of his performance. Goffman uses an anecdote from the school setting to illustrate the concept of dramatic realization. Borrowing from the writing of Sartre, Goffman recounts how students try to impress teachers by being extremely attentive. The student rivets his eyes on the teacher, his ears are open wide, so that he exhausts himself in playing the attentive role, and ends up by not actually hearing anything.[4]

To illustrate dramatic realization with the teacher giving the performance, we offer a description of an early childhood teacher who keeps a mirror in a stand on her piano. The mirror is arranged at an appropriate angle so the teacher can see her four-year-olds even though her back is turned to them while she plays the piano. As the children sing and request numbers, the teacher merely glances in the mirror to see whom to call on next. This teacher has developed the technique of *actually* being able to survey her pupils reactions even when her back is turned to them. As Goffman describes dramatic realization if the activity is to become significant to others, the performer must mobilize his actions *during the per-*

---

4. Ibid., p. 33.

formance in order to heighten what he wishes to portray. This individual provides dramatic realization of the role of the young child's teacher by being ever watchful (even in her mirror) of the needs, reactions, and feelings of her pupils.

Another term that describes performance in degree and kind is *idealization*. Idealized performances refer to those that fulfill the expectations of the society. When the individual presents himself to others he will tend to incorporate and exemplify the actions that the audience values and even admires for the particular role. Here Goffman discusses middle-class housewives who, among other performances, will set out appropriate magazines such as the *Family Circle* on their livingroom coffee tables while hiding their *True Romance* (or more recently *Cosmopolitan*) in the bedroom dresser drawer. So too, do some teachers of young children put on an idealized personal front as part of their performance of dedication to the job of tending and educating little children—though they do not give up the weekly 4 p.m. hair dresser's appointment!

Mystification also describes an aspect of the performance being given for the audience. Mystification involves maintaining social distance so that awe will be generated in the audience. This readily applies to the classic stereotype of the kindergarten teacher who traditionally has stood as an authority on all things pertaining to young children. Here the audience could be parents, the principal, and other lay personnel as well as the kindergarteners, who view Miss Brown, the kindergarten teacher, as the Oracle of Delphi.

THE SINCERE OR THE PHONY PERFORMANCE

Teachers of young children realize that their audience, their pupils, the parents, their colleagues—including the principal—really expect them to be knowledgeable and assured in the handling of very young children. This is considered a highly specialized task in our society, just as medicine and care of the mentally and emotionally ill are considered specialized tasks in our culture. Most of Goffman's anecdotal material comes from the medical profession, but teaching also offers meaningful situations for analysis by Goffman's sociological model.

Goffman points out that individuals engaging in a performance may be "sincere," that is, they may firmly believe that the impression they are creating represents the "real reality;" or they may be "cynical," that is, they have very little belief in their own act. Naturally, most performances are not totally one or the other extreme, but contain elements of both. He describes several conditions under which concealment of one's inadequacies takes place. Of these conditions, one applies particularly to teachers of young children. "We find that errors and mistakes are often corrected before the performance takes place, while telltale signs that errors have been made and corrected are themselves concealed. In this way an impression of infallibility, so important in many presentations, is maintained."[5]

Teachers of four-, five-, and six-year-olds develop a technique of bringing groups of noisy children to quiet attention in a few seconds by the playing of a chord on the piano and a simple finger play such as "open, shut them," or "hands on your head, hands in your lap." They do this with what seems miraculous ease to the visitor in the early childhood classroom. One minute 30 to 35 little bodies are scurrying about the room in noisy confusion. Next minute it seems one can "hear a pin drop." The casual visitor to the classroom, often the school principal, is amazed and awed at this outstanding performance of discipline and often remarks about it to others. The observer does not know of the days and months of "practice" that have gone into such a performance and the skill and attentiveness of the teacher in knowing just the crucial moment to play the chord and go into the routine before the children have gotten "out of hand."

In *Humanity and Modern Sociological Thought,* Professor Cuzzort brings new insights into the application of Goffman's theories to education.

> Concealment is a necessary element in practically all social performances, and it poses a rather trying dilemma for the actor. If he is honest and open, that is, if he refuses to engage in concealment, then he risks losing his audience. If he engages in concealment, then he is practicing deceit. All human social performances, from Goffman's perspective, involve a constant weighing of the costs of losing one's audience against the cost of losing one's integrity by behaving in a deceptive manner. . . . Goffman would suggest something different: "phony" behavior is a product of the relationship existing between the performer and those who observe him. If retention of the audience is important, then deceit may be necessary. Thus, the teacher who is committed to the ideal of educating youth can do so only by retaining the attention and the acceptance of the students who become his immediate concern. This can be achieved only through performances which convince the audience of the worth of the performer. Such performances will necessarily conceal errors, hidden pleasures, "dirty work," and tedium. On these occasions the performer often cannot escape the sense of deception that he is practicing.[6]

Hence, Cuzzort's description of concealment or the "phony" performance in the teaching profession applies extremely well to teachers of young children. Some kindergarten and nursery school teachers are sincerely convinced of their ability to cope with the education of pre-schoolers. They

---

5. Ibid., p. 43.
6. R. P. Cuzzort, *Humanity and Modern Sociological Thought* (New York: Holt, Rinehart & Winston, Inc., 1969), pp. 179–80.

conceal the errors, the mistakes, and certainly the tedious and routine nature of the job that requires continual patience and forebearance when dealing with young children. On the other hand, it is not unusual to hear the remark, "Oh, I am only a nursery school teacher," or "I'm *only* a kindergarten teacher," revealing a cynical view of one's effectiveness in dealing with very young children, and also, apparently the low prestige this job carries in the eyes of the audience.

Others Join in the Performance. The performer can function alone or be a member of a troupe or cast of players. Goffman defines a "performance team" as any set of individuals who cooperate in staging a single routine. He draws an example from family life in American society: "when a husband and wife appear before new friends for an evening of sociability, the wife may demonstrate more respectful subordination to the will and opinion of her husband than she may bother to show when alone with him or when with old friends. When she assumes a respectful role, he can assume a dominant one; and when each member of the marriage team plays its special role, the conjugal unit, as a unit, can sustain the impression that new audience expect of it."[7]

Another example comes from proper business etiquette. One addresses his co-workers in the office or his secretary by "Mr." or "Miss" (or "Ms.") when outsiders are present, although everyone in the office may be on a first name basis during the daily routine of activities. The school, elementary or secondary, is also a type of business setting. Teachers greet each other by their first names in the classroom, the hall, the office or the teachers' lounge when no children are present or at least within hearing. Yet, if a child appears on the scene it constitutes a breach of etiquette to refer to Miss Green, the art teacher, as "Blanche." One way to refer to a member of your clique or particular in-group on large school faculty is to refer to the individual always by their first name (before other teachers, *never* before the students) when that individual is not present but is mentioned in the conversation. These small, but really significant actions, reveal the subtleties of the "performance team": who are considered the members, who are labeled outsiders, or the audience for the team.

Performance teams are flexible and the cast of characters in the troupe can shift and change. There are times when the teacher and the students become a team and the outsiders or the audience can consist of parents, other teachers, supervisors, the principal, or other administrators. The writer is not referring to the traditional school performance situation, where mothers and fathers (if they are around) are invited to the kindergarten from 1:00 to 1:30 on Tuesday afternoon to see the rhythm band

---

7. Erving Goffman, *Presentation of Self,* pp. 70–79.

play several numbers just before Christmas. Rather let us look at a more subtle but commonplace situation in the public school setting. A teacher new to the system must be evaluated by superiors. It is known that the coordinator, supervisor, or principal will be coming around to observe the classroom. The teacher allies the students to perform in the manner that will be expected by the evaluator, even to the extent in some cases, that the threat of the teacher's classroom evaluation is used as a means of discipline for the pupils in the classroom. This is especially effective with young children. The teacher may say, "Oh, you know Mr. Brown, our principal, is coming in one of these days and he doesn't like to see messy tables and noisy children." And when the principal does arrive for a brief inspection, the cast of characters, children and teacher alike, are alerted to provide him with the performance he seems to be expecting.

What is being said here of the new teacher on the job, can also be used to characterize the student teacher, perhaps even more so. This writer has the opportunity to regularly supervise student teachers, particularly in several open-space elementary schools. In the setting of the open pod-style school, with 150 to 200 children in a large, carpeted space sectioned off by bulletin boards, a line of desks and chairs, many styles of dividers, or other devices, the supervisor can observe the candidate to be evaluated in a very casual and unobtrusive manner. Yet five- and six-year-olds in this setting, will look up from their reading or their project and remark that "Here comes the lady from the university to see if Miss —————— is teaching us all right." The children were alerted to the performance that was expected when the "outsider" arrived, by a member of their team, their student teacher.

The Setting for the Team. In describing the open-space school, where large groups of children—150 to 200 or more—are placed in a continuous space, with a team of teachers and assistants, anywhere from three or four to nine or ten adults, to supervise and direct the learning activities, Goffman's concepts of regions and "region behavior" come clearly to the fore. Goffman defines a region as "any place that is bounded to some degree by barriers to perception. Regions vary, of course, in the degree to which they are bounded and according to the media of communication in which the barriers to perception occur. Thus thick glass panels, such as are found in broadcasting control rooms, can isolate a region aurally but not visually, while an office bounded by beaverboard partitions is closed off in the opposite way."[8]

So also are regions set apart in open-space schools. We just described how various devices are used to delineate a specific region where

8. Ibid., p. 106.

this group or that group functions most of the time. Groups are usually designated by age levels in the open-space elementary school, especially when this type of organization is just evolving for the staff of a school. Teachers still hold to the grade-level designation. The tendency is to denote the first-grade level as located in this section, second grade over here, and so on. As the school staff becomes acclimated to the open-space setting, grade or age levels seem to drop away as designations for the groups of children and the labels may now be Pod A, B, C, or colors (red, green blue), or labels such as aspen, oak, elm, etc. Yet space is still subject to boundaries and barriers. The Instructional Materials Center with its book cases and carrels can form high walls to bound off specific areas where children of different ages function the majority of their school day.

In the traditional elementary school classroom, regions are usually designated, with the whole room being a specific region in the school, "Room 102" (the first grade) or specifically labeled "The First Grade." Just as traditionally the kindergarten has been constructed as a larger space with areas for a doll or housekeeping corner, tables and chairs area for seat work, an open space for rhythms near the piano, so are child-sized lavatories, drinking fountain, and sinks often included in the layout of the room. Early elementary school classrooms have been conventionally organized with the teacher's desk in the front of the room and rows of desks placed parallel to the windows, which usually run the length of the room. At the back are placed several long tables for displays and materials. Bookshelves and cupboards are on the walls opposite the windows. Chalk boards are on the walls behind the teacher's desk and at the rear. A bulletin board is usually in the corner beside the door that provides the entry to the classroom.

Regions can more easily be delineated in the traditional elementary school classroom, than in the traditional kindergarten and open space school. Most adroitly Goffman denotes a "front" and a "back region," where the team performs. In this dramaturgic model both the traditional school and the innovative open school can become settings with front and back regions. The "front" region is referred to as the place where the performance is given, while the "back" region is a place, relative to a given performance, where the impression fostered by the performance is knowingly contradicted as a matter of course.[9] The teachers' lounge would eminently qualify for the example of a back region. It is here that at times emotions are fully expressed, from sobbing declamations of failure to the exhilaration successful teaching can bring. Teachers of young children often feel the fatigue of being "on stage" for hours on end. In some situations the elementary school teacher's "day" can equal six to seven hours of un-

---

9. Ibid., p. 112.

Fig. 2.2. "I'm wearing my new boots"—self-portrait by Jamy, University Park Elementary School Kindergarten, Denver, Colorado. (Courtesy Kathleen Roth.)

relieved duty with children. Yet the teachers' lounge provides the backstage area where the adult can relax from the performance.

But do the children in the school have such a "back" region? The playground or out-of-doors sometimes functions in this way, but often this area is but another sector of the front region for teachers and students alike. Then we wonder why young children in the school setting become so restless and uncontrollable at the end of the day. There is really no back region for them. No place to let go and relax from pressures of the performance in school!

WHEN THE PERFORMANCE BECOMES BLEMISHED—STIGMAS

In a later work, *Stigma: Notes on the Management of Spoiled Identity,* Goffman delineates further extensions of his dramaturgic sociology. He presents the concept of stigma as an attribute that is deeply discrediting. A person with a stigma is not quite human. Hence the individual's performance becomes blemished by the stigma. Goffman writes:

> Three grossly different types of stigma may be mentioned. First there are abominations of body—the various physical deformities. Next there are blemishes of individual character perceived as weak will, domineering

Fig. 2.3. "A Portrait of Myself" by Kelley, University Park Elementary School Kindergarten, Denver, Colorado. (Courtesy Kathleen Roth.)

or unnatural passions, treacherous and rigid beliefs, and dishonesty, these being inferred from a known record of, for example, mental disorder, imprisonment, addiction, alcoholism, homosexuality, unemployment, suicidal attempts, and radical political behavior. Finally there are the tribal stigma of race, nation, and religion, these being stigma that can be transmitted through lineages and equally contaminate all members of a family.[10]

Those who do not depart negatively from particular expectations Goffman labels as "normals." In an amusing footnote he comments how questionable individuals such as criminals attempt to prove their claim to normalcy by citing how they are so devoted to their families that they spend every Christmas and Thanksgiving with them.

A sensitive and alert elementary school teacher used a sociological approach in studying two "blemished" students. In the following analysis

10. Erving Goffman, *Stigma: Notes on the Management of Spoiled Identity* (Englewood Cliffs, N.J.: Prentice-Hall, Inc., 1963), p. 3.

of the impact of stigma upon the lives of young children in school a new perspective—dramaturgic sociology—was employed by Janis Dithmer to understand the problems the individual encounters in his performance at school. (Parenthetical page references are to Goffman's *Stigma.*)

> The two characters about whom my essay is written tend to exemplify more than one of Goffman's classifications of stigma. They both may be said to have character blemishes; but in addition, they are a part of the tribal stigma of race. I must admit that my primary concern here is with the first category of character blemishes; but there are instances, to be cited later, where one stigma is quite inseparable from the other.
>
> Each person with a stigma experiences a unique pattern of development in life. Goffman calls this development his "moral career" (p. 32). The stigmatized reach a turning point where they can no longer be protected by their family and friends.
>
> Suddenly, as these individuals try to build social relationships with others, the undesirable attributes which they possess become evident. The first encounter of non-acceptance by peers may come with school entrance.
>
> This period or phase in the "moral career" of an individual with a stigma is the one toward which I will now focus my attention. The observations and ideas which will be presented are gleaned from a personal teaching experience. This experience took place in the third grade of a racially mixed elementary school. The two students who were (and probably still are) being stigmatized occupy opposite ends of the scale of intelligence—one being a slow learner, the other being a very bright and advanced learner. Although the majority of ostracism and non-acceptance was exhibited by other students, I do intend to discuss some evidence of these actions displayed by family members as well as the teacher.
>
> During the course of my reading, I have found that particularly the theories of three social scientists bear strong association to the very real problem I am about to discuss. Erving Goffman has developed some interesting theories regarding the nature of stigma as well as its consequences for both the individual and society. Jules Henry delves into the very deepest thoughts and feelings held by the stigmatized individual—those of the fear of failure and the fear of his enemies. Finally, Peter Berger has presented a theory explaining the actions of the so-called "normal human being." All society is governed by controls, and the mental punishment or ridicule experienced by the stigmatized is but a mechanism by which this control is enforced. As I discuss the two individual cases with which I had such personal involvement, it is my hope that the forceful relationship of these theories will become as clear to others as it is to me.
>
> **Jesse Johnson—"The Slow Learner."** The problem child in the classroom, the clown, the thief, the lazy and inattentive—to what may all of this be attributed? In the case of Jesse Johnson, an eight-year-old Negro student, one may say that he is a child with a stigma. This stigma has resulted from failure to learn or achieve. The group of

"normal" children with whom he must try to affiliate may label him "dumb" or "stupid," the educator may label him a "slow learner" but the individual must suffer the consequences. This stigma has placed Jesse in a category where expectations of the role he should play make him unacceptable to the group. As he is pushed out, the anxieties and frustrations which he feels serve only to deepen a rather serious problem.

According to Goffman, all of those who are stigmatized have an individual pattern of life development, a "moral career" involving their particular stigma. Before this career begins, the child is protected by his family—in Jesse's case by his mother. It is my feeling that this period of protection was the major reason for the ensuing stigma. Because of ignorance, not lack of concern, Jesse was not given the opportunity for experiences so vital to the development of mental processes. I learned from the kindergarten teacher that he had never owned scissors, crayons or pencil; and he had never had cutting and pasting experiences before entering school. In addition, his impressions of the natural environment were very limited. After actual confrontations with Mrs. Johnson, I realized that she herself had very poor comprehensive abilities; and after sending messages back and forth between home and school, I realized that her reading and writing skills were also rather restricted. Thus, Jesse began school with an existing stigma that might possibly have been avoided.

Erving Goffman sees the term stigma in the light of two perspectives—the stigmatized individual who perceives that his differentness is evident to those with whom he is in interaction; and the stigmatized individual who assumes that it is not known about by those in the group nor necessarily obvious to them. Goffman refers to this first group as the "discredited," and to the second group as the "discreditable." As these two terms are not always inseparable, it becomes quite difficult to assign one of them to this student. Instead, as a tennis ball lands on first one side of the net then the other, so does Jesse bounce back and forth within the realm of these groups. At the time of school entrance before continuous social interaction had begun, one may have placed him among the "discreditable." Then, as his classmates became "mixed contacts"—placing the stigmatized and the normal in the same social situation, they began to discover his weaknesses. At this point, Jesse would have been placed within the "discredited" group. But the cycle does not stop here. I can remember several unique occurrences, when for some unknown reason, Jesse was able to participate as a "normal" in an activity. For example, on at least two of our spelling tests he was able to spell correctly over one-half of the words given. On these occasions, Jesse's placement within one or the other of the two categories would have been quite difficult.

Regardless of whether the stigmatized is "discreditable" or "discredited," he must decide what plan of action he will follow in order to obscure or at least minimize his differentness. According to Goffman, there are several responses which the stigmatized might use to alter his situation. First, he may make a direct attempt to change that part of his character (or physical handicap, depending upon the kind of stigma which he has) which he sees to be different. Second, he can, in privacy, attempt to indirectly master those areas that are ordinarily closed to a person with his stigma. Finally, the individual may present himself in an unrealistic, unconventional manner which breaks with the social identity he now has.

Jesse Johnson, during his third year in school, chose the last plan. At this point, he perceived that the only possible way to become an accepted member of the group would be to hide his failings, to "fake" success, or as Goffman labels it—"to pass." He attempted this "front" in many ways. Goffman calls this form of response "dramatic realization." Not only did Jesse wish to be attentive, but he also waved his hand furiously as if he knew the answer to every question asked. Another means used by Jesse when asked a question to which he did not know the answer was to give the appearance of being deeply absorbed in his work. But with all performers, certain situations do arise where he will pass on to someone else in the group that he is only maintaining an act. Such was the case with Jesse as he gave a cockeyed glance or a snickering smile to one of his classmates in the back of the room. Interestingly enough, when Goffman's "back region" or "backstage"—where the impression of a performance may be contradicted—such as in an individual reading group, Jesse once again became himself. It was during these periods, when he was not "on," that Jesse made the most progress in learning.

In discussing the consequences of attempted "passing," Goffman identifies several personal reactions which he feels might affect the supersensual state of the stigmatized. To begin, he will most likely develop a rather high-grade feeling of anxiety—he may be exposed, and his life may collapse instantly. Second, the individual may be torn between his own group and the group he is pretending to be a part of. In other words, he may feel that there is more protection and security in his own group, but more possibility of need fulfillment in this new one. Finally, he may have to be very alert to certain aspects of social interaction which "normals" handle automatically; for example, forcing attentiveness when not really interested or able to comprehend what is being said (p. 87).

Perhaps one more very significant consequence of being stigmatized, whether attempting to pass or not, has been identified by Jules Henry. The individual, knowing that he has some differentness, some weakness, experiences the constant nightmare of the fear of failure. (See Jules Henry, *Culture Against Man* [New York: Random House, 1962], p. 300.) In Jesse's case, each time that he came before the class and was unable to give the correct response, the nightmare of failure became a reality. Because of our culture, the most likely response to failure is self-hatred. Such a poor image of one's self leads not to success, which is what the person with a stigma must find, but to more nonfulfillment.

At this point, I have discussed only the feelings and actions of the person with a stigma. It seems also necessary to look at the other side of the coin and to find some explanation for the attitudes held by the so-called "normals." I turn again to Jules Henry, as he sees the development of stigma to be a product of our culture. He applies this within the framework of our educational system, where culture teaches children that the "proper" attitude is to feel pleasure with another's failure (see Henry, p. 291). Thus, those who consistently fail, such as Jesse Johnson, are set apart as the stigmatized. Unless he can aptly maintain his performance, he is faced with the possibility of loss of group membership and group affection.

At this particular point the "moral career" of Jesse Johnson seems rather clouded. The stigma which he has remains; the course of action which he has chosen to combat the stigma seems only to intensify his anxieties. Henry feels that the stigmatized child must look for "impulse release" within the family, but Jesse is not afforded this opportunity. Not only is his mother unable to comprehend his problem, but her own stigma of belonging to a minority group seems to be much more worthy of her time. Perhaps in the future, as he looks and experiments with a new plan to action to minimize his stigma, Jesse will find more self-understanding and self-acceptance.

Charles Broadus—"The Bright Student." When a student possessing a high level and range of abilities is placed within a group whose skills are average to low-average, interaction becomes a problem. Perhaps an individual may become bored with the conversations of his class-mates, or bored with the material being presented. Perhaps the other students may become annoyed with the individual's lack of interest and apparent success. Perhaps the educator may feel some jealousy toward the child, as he probably can relate more information on a particular topic than she can—especially on an elementary level where the teacher merely scratches the surface in the various subject areas. All of these attitudes contribute to the development of a stigma which must evoke some response by the stigmatized.

Such was the case with Charles Broadus, an eight-year-old Negro child who occupied a very difficult position in my classroom. As with Jesse Johnson, Charles had an "undesired differentness" which prohibited group acceptance. Even the gap between "virtual social identity"—the character we give to an individual, and "actual social identity"—the character which he probably possesses can be shown to have existed (p. 2). In reconsidering Goffman's kinds of stigma, one may see that the two boys fall within the same group—that of individuals with character blemishes. This, however, is where the similarity ends. The anxieties which Charles experienced were not so much a result of non-acceptance by his class-mates, but rather a feeling that he could not successfully become part of any group. Intellectually, his ideas seemed to parallel those of students who were several years older, but emotionally he was not mature enough to become involved in their social activities.

Charles Broadus, being a stigmatized individual, has also had a pattern of development, or "moral career" regarding his differentness. As discussed previously, many children are protected by their families before school entrance; thus, they do not really know whether or not they conform to the standards set by society. This protection, as seen through Jesse, can be the major cause of the eventual stigma. When the family deliberately sets out to show the child that he is different— that he is superior—then the stigma begins in the home rather than as a result of it. Such is the case with Charles. Both his mother and his father are well-educated and intellectual. I have learned, from informal conversations with them, that they wish their son to realize that he is capable of achieving much more than other children. Not only are they extremely conscious of the intelligence factor, but also the idea that the one who is bright is a member of a racial minority. Consequently, entering school did not provide a particular turning point for Charles. Instead, as he searched for a place within a group, the gap between what his parents had taught him to believe about himself and what his deepest feelings were seemed to widen.

Of Goffman's two perspectives or ways of looking at those with a stigma, it seems that one may be most appropriately applied to a bright student with a pattern of development similar to that discussed above. Specifically Charles, whose life has been centered around the attribute which he holds, may be identified as a "discredited" individual. To restate the meaning of the term, an individual may be labeled "discredited" if he perceives that the differentness which he possesses is known about by those with whom he makes contact in interaction. In contrast to Jesse, whose career has shifted within the realm of both the "discredited" and the "discreditable," Charles has maintained stability. Interestingly enough, being exposed to one group or another has not provided the major frustration. This has come from having the ability to understand a situation qualitatively by manipulating many associations, yet understanding has not provided a place or group where he would fit comfortably.

As with all stigmatized individuals, this one had to decide on a plan—a way of responding to his situation. Though he did not attempt to "pass" or fake average or low abilities, Charles did employ a form of behavior which broke with reality and which was an unconventional cast of his character. Typically, he became conceited and smug when any job was placed before him. In addition, he was very openly intolerant of those less able to achieve. Quite significant, however, is the fact that when placed in a position of responsibility, such as working with Jesse individually, he exhibited a great amount of kindness and patience. In other words, in a situation where Charles felt comfortable and protected (which I might add he did not experience at home) he felt no need to convey feelings of superiority.

The consequences for a child with this particular stigma are steep. Emotionally, he is not able to live up to the role expectations which his parents have placed upon him. He has implanted Henry's constant "nightmare of the fear of failure." His self-image is crowded with feelings of ambivalence. Most dreadful is the thought that he does not have a group of intimates to whom he may turn for "impulse release."

We see our society bounded by certain stereotypes of what the "normal" individual should be. Anyone straying from such boundaries enters into the realm of the stigmatized. As a result, he is unable to develop satisfying interpersonal relations which are so important to the fulfillment of human needs. In addition, the individual formulates poor personal attitudes which may lead to self-hatred. To be placed in such a group, as Goffman says we all have been at one time or another in our lifetime, is a serious threat to existence. When this is experienced

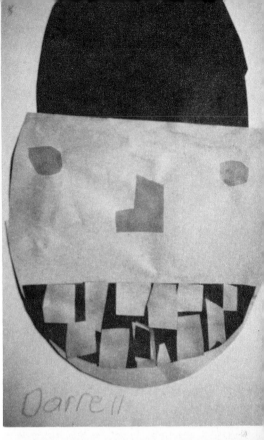

Figs. 2.4, 2.5, 2.6. "The Nightmare Fears of Failure" — self-portraits from construction paper by emotionally maladjusted seven-year-olds. (Courtesy Richard Dovenberg.)

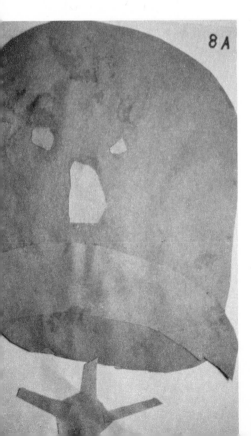

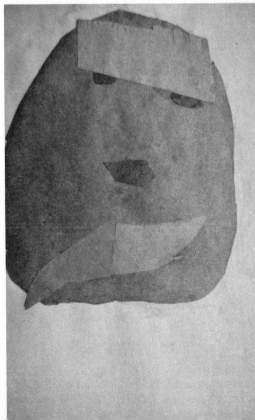

by a young child, it may so affect him as to indelibly dictate his future. Though he may survive physically, he has died emotionally.[11]

From this account we see how casting the classroom into the dramaturgic model gives the teacher new insights and perspectives on the impact of schooling in the lives of young children.

AN EXTENSION OF STIGMA — THE CHILD IN SPECIAL EDUCATION

When young children in public schools indicate their inability to perform in the group of "normals," special categories are set up by educators to channel these children into educational programs that can accommodate their "learning disabilities." Once again we bring the powerful and searching mechanism of dramaturgic sociology to examine what the categorization of "special education" can mean in the life of the child. Fred Resh, school psychologist and staff member of the Special Education Program at the University of Denver, employs Goffman's concepts of stigma, blemishes, and society's techniques for adaption to failure for the child labeled "special ed."

> Equality of educational opportunity is a pressing problem in all metropolitan areas, and recent legal decisions have amplified the problem even more. Tracking systems, which serve to perpetuate segregation, and the discriminatory use of IQ tests, can no longer be justified. How can the educational establishment cope with the gigantic problem presented to it by the inner city? Most educators will agree that general education has failed the black ghetto child. In an effort to avoid the necessity of radically changing the general education system in the black ghetto, the educational establishment has found it expedient to turn to special education, to greatly expand the special education programs serving black children. What this effectively does is label a disproportionate number of black and other minority children as retarded, disturbed, and/or delinquent. By means of this labeling process, the general educational enterprise is allowed to evade the responsibility for its failure to adapt to the needs of its black clientele, i.e., "How can we be expected to educate these children who are retarded and emotionally disturbed? They obviously belong in Special Education classes." This process effectively shortcircuits change in the general education program by implicating the children rather than the system.
>
> The relationship between the regular and general education systems in this case can be understood in terms of Goffman's concept of "cooling the mark out." Goffman takes this concept from the underworld of the confidence game and expands it to meaningfulness in many common

11. Janis Dithmer, "Stigma: Its Development and Consequences for the School Age Child" (unpublished paper submitted to graduate course in Educational Sociology, Spring, 1971, School of Education, University of Denver).

social situations. (See Erving Goffman, "On Cooling the Mark Out: Some Aspects of Adaption to Failure," *Psychiatry* 15 (1952): 443-51.)

The "mark" is the victim of a confidence game, the "sucker." The typical confidence game, or "con," consists of the following phases: The potential sucker is first spotted, and one member of the team, the "steerer," makes contact with him. The confidence of the mark is won, and he is given an opportunity to invest his money in a gambling venture which he understands to be fixed in his favor. The mark is permitted to win some money, then persuaded to invest more. Then there is an "accident," or mistake, and the mark loses his total investment. The con men thereupon depart, in a ceremony called the "blowoff." They leave the mark, but take his money. The mark is expected to go his way, a little wiser and a lot poorer.

Sometimes, however, a mark is not prepared to accept his loss. He may feel moved to complain, to call the police, to "beef" or "squawk." From the operator's point of view this would be bad for business, since it would alert other potential marks to the real nature of the con. In the event this occurs, an additional phase must be at the end of the game. This is called, "cooling the mark out." After the blowoff has occurred, one of the operators stays with the mark and makes an effort to keep his anger within sensible and manageable limits. The "cooler" exercises the art of consolidation. He defines the situation in such a way as to make it easy for the mark to accept his loss, his failure, and go quietly home.

Goffman broadens the definition of mark to include persons whose expectations or self-concepts have been shattered. These persons must be helped to re-accept themselves and their failure, and build a new framework for judging themselves. For example, with regard to a situation in which a person has failed at a job, he can be offered another position which differs from the one he has lost, but provides at least a something or a somebody to become. Thus, the feeling of failure is softened, the loser is pacified and resigned to his loss. The lover may be asked to become a "good friend," the poor parish priest may be transferred to a monastery, the losing boxer may be asked to become a trainer, the losing football coach, a physical education director. In the educational world, the failing student of medicine may be told he would make a good podiatrist, the failure in academically oriented high school classes may be advised to switch to a general education program.

Let us apply the concept of "cooling the mark out" in more detail to the relationship between general and special education. General education, by definition, is supposed to be capable of teaching all children. But when confronted with inner city black children, it has failed. Given the traditional methodology of the public schools, both white and Negro teachers have found themselves impotent when it comes to educating increasing numbers of black children. One method by which these educators and their school systems can preserve their identities is by cooling deviant children out. Special education programs are mandated on the basis that the new placement will help the child. In essence, he is given a seemingly better placement in hopes that he will stop putting up a fuss. It is easier for all to cool out the child, to help

Figs. 2.7, 2.8. Construction-paper self-portraits by children with severe learning disabilities, seven-year-old boys of Mexican-American background. (Courtesy Richard Dovenberg.)

him and his parents accept his failure in the regular education system, than it is to change that system for his benefit.

Special education, then, is part of the arrangement for cooling out students who won't conform to traditional classroom methodology. It has aided in erecting a parallel system which permits relief of institutional guilt and humiliation stemming from failure to achieve competence and effectiveness in the educational task given by society. Special education is helping the regular school maintain its spoiled identity when it creates special programs for the "disruptive child," the "emotionally disturbed child," or the "mildly retarded child," most of whom happen to be black, poor, and live in the inner city! [12]

Minority Affiliation as Stigma. Resh has underscored how the label "special education," "emotionally disturbed," "mentally retarded" can be used by a school district to segregate and hence undereducate minority group children. The writer will cite two examples which illustrate this situation. In one case, the minority group are black children; in the other, the group of children singled out for the special education channel are Mexican-American. In the instance of the special education classes mainly populated by black, disadvantaged youngsters, the school district is located in the Midwest of the United States in a vast urban area. For many years and up until recently the "Special A" and "Special B" classes were largely made up of black children labeled disruptive, mentally retarded, unruly, unman-

---

12. Fred Resh, "Is Special Education A Form of 'Cooling The Mark Out?' An Application of Goffman's Theories in Education" (unpublished, Fall, 1970), pp. 1–4.

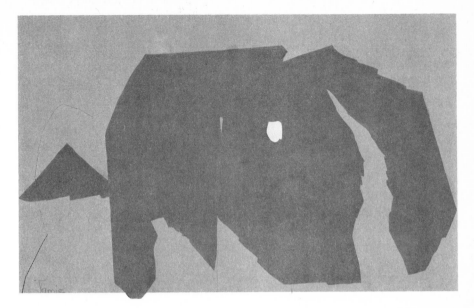

Fig. 2.9. Self-portrait by disturbed five-year-old Mexican-American boy. (Courtesy Beverly Gonzalez.)

ageable, etc. When a substitute was called to come to an elementary school in this district for the day, the technique for advising him or her of the difficulties of the position to be filled, was by indicating that there was, or there was not, a "Special A" in that school. This was a subtle and indirect means of informing the substitute teacher of the socioeconomic, ethnic, or racial composition of the student body of that particular school.

In the case of the second school district, located in one of the largest cities of the American Southwest, children of Mexican-American heritage were found almost exclusively in a special track of the school system created for slow learners and leading with amazing regularity to school dropouts by eighth grade or school leaving age of about 13 years.

Another interesting aspect of the placement of special education classes in elementary schools is the emergence of new trends now that more open space, team teaching, individualized learning schools are springing up. When specialized services for children with learning disabilities and emotional problems are incorporated in open space, ungraded schools these children are not so obviously segregated from the "normals." Their status as blemished learners is not so easily recognized by other children and teachers. In one open-space school known to the writer, the teacher handling the special education classes has made heroic efforts to continually integrate the children with learning disabilities into the groupings of "normal" children. She has noted the progress and exceptionally optimistic attitudes displayed by her students, and by their parents as well. It seems that the child labeled "special education" not only learns to question his self-worth at an early age, but his parents, also, deem him blemished and his school career bound for failure almost from the start. When such children with spoiled identities can be integrated into well organized open space school their chances of overcoming their learning disabilities are apt to increase manyfold.

THE REALIZATION OF STIGMA IN THE YOUNG CHILD

Goffman makes reference on a number of occasions in his writings of the realization of blemishment early in the individual's life. He writes that the orphan learns that children naturally and normally have parents, even while he is learning what it means not to have any. And when a child begins public school this may be the occasion of his learning about his particular stigma from the taunting, teasing, and ostracism that results from his presence in the new group. From a remarkable and moving account of a kindergarten founded in 1889 comes this touching story of Patsy. Written by Kate Douglas Wiggin and published by Houghton, Mifflin and Company in 1894, this story of a crippled, orphan boy, Patsy, was written and sold for the benefit of the Silver Street Free Kindergartens in San Francisco during the 1890s. Kate Wiggin's description of the first meeting with Patsy illustrates so well this early recognition of stigma and blemished identity, that we quote it in its entirety.

> A boy, seeming—how many years old shall I say? for in some ways he might have been a century old when he was born—looking, in fact as if he had never been young, and would never grow older. He had a shrunken, somewhat deformed body, a curious, melancholy face, and such a head of dust-colored hair that he might have been shocked for a doormat. The sole redeemers of the countenance were two big, pathetic, soft dark eyes, so appealing that one could hardly meet their glance without feeling instinctively in one's pocket for a biscuit or a ten-cent piece. But such a face! He had apparently made an attempt at a toilet without the aid of a mirror, for there was a clear circle like a racetrack round his nose, which member reared its crest untouched and grimy, from the centre, like a sort of judge's stand, while the dusky rim outside represented the space for audience seats.
>
> I gazed at this astonishing diagram of a countenance for a minute, spellbound, thinking it resembled nothing so much as a geological map, marked with coal deposits. And as for his clothes, his jacket was ragged and arbitrarily docked at the waist, while one of his trousers-legs was slit up at the side, and flapped hither and thither when he moved, like a lug-sail in a calm.

"Well, sir," said I at length, waking up to my duties as hostess, "did you come to see me?"

"Yes, I did."

"Let me think; I don't seem to remember; I am so sleepy. Are you one of my little friends?"

"No, I hain't yit, but I'm goin' to be."

"That's good, and we'll begin right now, shall we?"

"I knowed yer fur Miss Kate the minute I seen yer."

"How was that, eh?"

"The boys said as how you was a kind o' pretty lady, with towzly hair in front." (Shades of my cherished curls!)

"I'm very obligated to the boys."

"Kin yer take me in?"

"What? Here? Into the Kindergarten?"

"Yes, I bin waitin' this yer long whiles fur to git in."

"Why, dear little boy," gazing dubiously at his contradictory countenance, "you're too-big, aren't you? We have only tiny little people here, you know; not six years old. You are more, aren't you?"

"Well I'm nine by the book; but I ain't more'n scerce six along o' my losing them three years."

"What do you mean, child? How could you *lose* three years?" cried I, more and more puzzled by my curious visitor.

"I lost 'em on the back stairs, don't yer know. My father he got fightin' mad when he was drunk and pitched me down two flights of 'em and my back was most clearn broke in two, so I couldn't git out o' bed forever, till just now."

"Why, poor child, who took care of you?"

"Mother she minded me when she warn't out washin'."

"And did she send you here to-day?"

"Well! however could she, bein' as how she's dead? I s'posed you knowed that. She died after I got well; she only waited for me to git up, anyhow."

O God! these poor mothers! they bite back the cry of their pain, and fight death with love so long as they have a shred of strength for the battle!

"What's your name, dear boy?"

"Patsy"

"Patsy, what?"

"Patsy nothin'! just only Patsy; that's all of it. The boys call me 'Humpty Dumpty' and 'Rags' but that's sassy." [13]

As the story develops Pasty joins the Silver Street Kindergarten and proves to be an invaluable as well as endearing aid to Miss Kate, the teacher. Toward the end of the school year Patsy develops a fatal illness and the book closes with the scene of Patsy on his death bed, as poignant and touching as any in the literature. Miss Kate sings a hymn and recites a little prayer as the dying child with gasps of his last breath, sighs, "I've got

---

13. Kate Douglas Wiggin, *The Story of Patsy* (Boston: Houghton, Mifflin Co., 1894), pp. 12–16.

Fig. 2.10. "I'm wearing my peace symbol"—five-year-old at Westwood School Kindergarten, Denver, Colorado. (Courtesy Beverly Gonzalez.)

enough o' this, I tell yer, with backaches, 'nd fits, 'nd boys callin' sassy names—'nd no gravy on my pertater;—but I hate to go'way from the Kindergartent—only p'raps Heaven is just like, only bigger, 'nd more children—Sing about the pleasant mornin' light, will yer, please—Miss Kate?"[14]

SOME NEW PERSPECTIVES IN TEACHING YOUNG CHILDREN

Whether we dip back into the descriptions of school life almost a century ago or focus on the latest in open-space schooling, still the power and potential of the sociological perspective brings new insights and new organization to the educational scene. In this chapter we have used the theories and concepts of dramaturgic sociology, mainly those developed by

14. Ibid., p. 66.

Erving Goffman, to study the interaction between students and teachers. We have drawn upon analogies and incidents in classrooms of young children and with teachers of young children to illustrate Goffman's concepts in dramaturgic sociology. These new perspectives in early childhood education tend to emphasize the emotional and social life that is a part of schooling, that hidden curriculum, the experience of schooling. The theatrical approach of dramaturgic sociology enables us to see the view from the individual's position, as well as the broader scene where groups of people and the values and attitudes of the wider society come into play and influence the actors. This new direction in sociological theory, dramaturgic sociology, provides the educator with exciting research techniques for understanding the process of education.

In the next chapter we will consider the broader societal values and attitudes, the processes of socialization and enculturation, that shape the child's personality and intellect. It is this dynamic interaction of society upon the individual, in the family, in the school, in the neighborhood, through the mass media that informs the child, early in his life, of his position and status in his group.

Fig. 2.11. "Nothing But Swinging" — five-year-old, University Park Elementary School Kindergarten, Denver, Colorado. (Courtesy Kathleen Roth.)

Sources

Cuzzort, R. P. *Humanity and Modern Sociological Thought*. New York: Holt
Rinehart & Winston, Inc., 1969.
Goffman, Erving. *Presentation of Self in Everyday Life*. Garden City, N. Y.:
Doubleday and Co. , 1959.
——————. *Stigma: Notes on the Management of Spoiled Identity*. Engle-
wood Cliffs, N. J.: Prentice-Hall, Inc., 1963.
Gouldner, Alvin. *The Coming Crisis in Western Sociology*. New York: Basic
Books, 1970.
Henry, Jules. *Culture Against Man*. New York: Random House, 1962.

chapter 3

The Socialization Process in the Young Child's Classroom

Most adults in American society have highly selective recollections of their childhood socialization. When asked to recall some of the most embarrassing or the most exciting moments of their childhood, especially events related to early school experience, they will focus on one or two specific events, often idealizing the situation and the characters involved. This selective memory process tends to limit the adult's understandings of the child's views of his world and of his early school experience. In her final volume published posthumously, Mary Ellen Goodman, the outstanding expert on cross-cultural studies of children, states:

> Among Americans the underestimation fallacy flourishes and undermines the intuitive insights of wise parents and teachers. The problem is the inability of many adults to appreciate the extent of a child's perceptions, his ability to understand interpersonal relations, and his ability to cope with frustrations, tensions, and troubles. It is true that his perceptions, understandings, and his ability to handle his emotions and problems are likely to differ both qualitatively and quantitatively from those of the adult. The child's lesser ability to verbalize will of itself reduce the fullness and clarity of his communications, if not of his conceptualizations. But the differences are of degree, not of kind.[1]

Goodman studied four- and five-year-olds in America and Japan over a period of three decades. She was a gifted and learned anthropologist, and wrote with an extensive knowledge of the anthropological literature on childhood socialization in cultures and societies, both folkish and sophisticated, around the globe. She writes that she has seen for herself how keen are the perceptions and how sharp the logic of children as they bring to bear on the social scene that which they have noted about people, things,

---

1. Mary Ellen Goodman, *The Culture of Childhood: Child's-Eye Views of Society and Culture* (New York: Teachers College Press, Columbia 1970), p. 3.

The Sad Little Girl

Once there was a sad little girl. She was sad and did'nt have any friends. The one girl that she met was too mean. She was a bad bad girl. The sad girl did'nt like her. Because she was the saddest girl in her class room. One day she met a lot of children then she was the happiest in her class. The End

By LILLIAN VIGIL

Fig. 3.1. "The Sad Little Girl"—Mesa Elementary School, Westminster, Colorado. (Courtesy Susan Levin.)

and behavior. And children arrive at, or try our, classifications on the basis
of these perceptions.

Take for example this delightful comment about his family and their
roles in the world of work from a six-year-old:

> Father teaches education, which is a service. My father teaches
> at McKee Hall. My father's name is_____.
>
> My mother is *just* a housewife but she tries to help with school
> problems. My mother produces services. She is very nice. Her name
> is_____.
>
> My sister doesn't produce anything but trouble. Her name is
> _____.

Or this comment from six-year-old Mark: "My dad is a teacher that
teaches teachers to be teachers."

A five-and-half-year-old writes: "My dad Dean of ares (sic) and
sinces (sic) he came up the hard way. First wen we came to G_____ he
was a teacher then he did another job. Then he became Dean."

These children, who attend a laboratory school on a college campus,
show keen perceptions about the social, economic, and political life of the
adult world that surrounds them. As Goodman so succinctly puts it, "It
must be remembered too that the child's knowledge will reflect the nature
and complexity of the total society and culture in which he finds himself.
Small folkish societies bearing nonliterature cultures present children a
comparatively narrow range of possibilities and alternatives. In large
urban-industrial societies bearing sophisticated and complex cultures the
range is wide."[2]

SEXUAL STEREOTYPES START EARLY

If young children are highly aware of the social life that goes on in their
midst, then they are certainly cognizant of the sex role behavior that is
appropriate in the culture. Florence Howe writes:

> Children learn about sex roles very early in their lives, probably before
> they are eighteen months old, certainly long before they enter school.
> They learn these roles through relatively simple patterns that most of
> us take for granted. We throw boy-babies up in the air and rough-house
> with them. We coo over girl-babies and handle them delicately. We
> choose sex-related colors and toys for our children from their earliest
> days. We encourage the energy and physical activity of our sons, just
> as we expect girls to be quieter and more docile. We love both our sons
> and daughters with equal fervor, we protest, and yet we are disappointed
> when there is no male child to carry on the family name.[3]

2. Ibid., p. 4.
3. Florence Howe, "Sex Stereotypes Start Early," *Saturday Review,* October 16, 1971,
p. 76.

So when her teacher asks her "What will you be when you grow up?" we find that six-year-old Rosemary writes:

I can be a mother.
I can be a (sic) actress.
I can be a wife and my name will be Rosemary Something.

This six-year-old female child in American culture is already aware that she gives up her surname for the name of the man she marries. Further this child seems to have been socialized very early into the sex-role stereotypes of American society. The popular Hallmark book for children *What Girls Can Be* tells us that women become housewives, mothers, nurses, actresses, models, teachers, or possibly artists. (Dean Wolley, *What Girls Can Be,* illus. E. Kornfeind, Kansas City: Hallmark Cards, Inc. not dated). The matched book in this set, *What Boys Can Be,* informs children that boys grow up to be policemen, firemen, astronauts, and maybe even President!

How often does it occur in kindergarten and even in nursery schools, that the girls will sit to the side while the boys move chairs and blocks or doll house furniture? How frequently do teachers of young children plan rhythmic activities with the galloping for boys only and the tiptoeing for girls only? Florence Howe continues her article on the education of women in America by noting that a substantial portion of the blame for the rein-forcement of sexual stereotypes should be placed with public education, even though it is true that the schools reflect the values and attitudes of the society they serve.

In describing the role of the school in the socialization of the young, Ronald Lippitt, social psychologist, feels that the school has been delegated a tremendously complex variety of socialization tasks. He lists these socialization tasks in broad categories:

> stimulating and guiding the unfolding of cognitive development,
> acquisition of information about past, present, and future,
> social-emotional growth and development,
> movement toward the selection and preparation for occupational and sex roles,
> nurturance of physical health,
> development of leisure-time interests,
> development of motivation and skills in the area of citizenship.

On the one hand, the school receives far too little in the way of collabora-tion from other segments of the community and far too much criticism for failure to achieve idealized standards; but on the other hand, it is typically very backward in utilizing the resources of social research and theory to improve its functioning as a subsystem of the community, as an organization, and as an association of small groups, called class-rooms, engaged in a program of interaction between adults and children, committed to the achievement of certain educational objectives.[4]

THE CHILD COPES WITH SOCIALIZING AGENTS

Not only does the school have a vastly complex task of socializing the individual, but the child, as well, is constantly bombarded by the impact of influencers. Lippitt characterizes these influences as competing inputs being thrust upon the child as a consumer. The child can assume several differing postures in order to cope with these influencers. One way for the child to cope with material or the learning situation being thrust upon him is to attend to the teacher or other influencer, at that moment, nodding and agreeing or giving the appearance of listening to the teacher. This is not unlike a situation we described in chapter 2, where the student attends so conscientiously he really doesn't hear what is said. However, in this case, which Lippitt terms the "compartmentalized solution" or "situational opportunism," the child copes with his socializer by attending only for the moment. First this adult is attempting to influence him, then another adult will tell an opposing "truth". The child will nod and agree in each instance with little attempt at personal decision-making or internal commitment to the proposition. This posture is probably characteristic of very young children, but also it applies especially well to the situation of the child from the inner city ghetto. In the school setting, the child is socialized with the values of middle-class, white America, while in the home setting different values and attitudes are being presented. The child tends to compartmentalize these messages about his culture in order to cope with them: *this* attitude is appropriate in the school situation; *this* one for the streets; *this* one for the home.

This philosophy was actually built into a language program for inner city, black children in the first grades of a large, Midwestern city school system. Children were taught that in school you speak one dialect of American English, while at home you speak another dialect of the language with your family. Both ways of talking, they were told, were equally valid and did the job of communicating, but one way was the language of the school and the other was your way of talking at home. Of course the problem with this type of thinking was that in actuality there was a great difference between the two dialects. The language of middle-class, American English was far more acceptable in the economic, political and social life of America than the disparaged dialect of the black ghetto. So the influences

---

4. Ronald Lippitt, "Improving the Socialization Process," in *Socialization and Society,* ed. John Clausen (Boston: Little, Brown and Co., 1968), p. 371.

from the school setting were not realistic in their presumptions that any dialect was equally as acceptable for functioning in our complex society.

Another way to cope with an array of socializers is to adopt a stance of a pervasive dominant loyalty. This posture, Lippitt indicates, is a method of simplifying the problem by making one reference group or one figure the dominant loyalty and behavioral guide across all situations, hence blocking out, rejecting, or withdrawing from other competing voices.[5]

A stunning example of this posture is portrayed in the film "Black History: Lost, Stolen or Strayed" (Of Black America Series, no. 1, 1968). The film depicts four-year-olds in a store-front school in Philadelphia being inculcated with the black heritage and hence prepared for attendance in the public schools. The black, male teacher shouts at the children, "What are you?" and they reply "Black and bee-u-ti-full!" over and over again. The teacher shouts, "No, you are not!" The children reply to him, shouting, "I am an Afro-American, I am black and I am beautiful!" The film indicates that this is a daily exercise in this store-front school for young blacks being prepared to enter the public school kindergarten. It seems apparent that these children would enter the public school with a pervasive dominant loyalty orientation to cope with the socializers they encounter. Further-more this coping posture could prove disasterous for the child entering a kindergarten with children of mixed ethnic backgrounds or encountering teachers who are not fully cognizant of his recent socializing experiences.

Still a third coping posture is that of "striking a balance." Lippitt de-scribes this stance as one of finding compromises, doing school work but also meeting the demands of friends or family. A charming anecdote to describe this posture is the story about the first grader who when encounter-ing the word "something" in the Dick and Jane story "Something Funny" could not seem to master or even understand this word to his teacher's puzzlement. The teacher repeated the term over and over again, "some-thing, some-thing." All of a sudden the child's eyes brightened up and his face broke into a big smile, "Oh you mean *sumpin'*!" came the response, and he proceeded to read the story now with meaning and some empathy. Here with merely a word, this child from a lower-class home had made the compromise between the terminology of the school and the peer group: "something" just meant "sumpin" in his way of speaking.

The fourth solution the child might seek in coping with forces that are attempting to socialize him, could be called "a-plague-on-all-your-houses,"

5. Ronald Lippitt. "The Neglected Receiver: The Child" in *Social Science in the Schools: A Search for Rationale,* edited by I. Morrissett and W. W. Stevens, Jr. (New York: Holt, Rinehart & Winston, Inc., 1971), pp. 172-84. In this reading Professor Lippitt outlines the postures described, but the present author has provided the illustrations and further applications of these concepts to the situation of the young child.

the rejection of all external authority pressures. Among young children this posture is expressed in extreme negativism— "no, no" in response to all requests. When children are four or five years of age the adult, who has been exposed to some child psychology, is wont to attribute such behavior to the extension of the rebelliousness of typical toddler stage of development. The teacher might label the highly negativistic five-or even six-year-old in the group as immature, still going through the "no, no I won't" stage, while in actuality this child is expressing the posture "a-plague-on-all-your-houses" in coping with the many forces that are attempting to socialize him. "This withdrawal from the influence arena receive support from the child's need for autonomy, from his negative feelings about authority, and from the attractiveness of the inner pleasure-seeking voices."[6]

Lippitt goes on to point out that even though we are focusing more than ever on the problems of socializing the young, our total educational effort is still one in which motivation is discouragingly low and learning opportunities are squandered—one of the most tragic wastes of human resources in our culture.

HOW UNIVERSAL ARE PRACTICES OF CHILD SOCIALIZATION?

At the conclusion of *The Culture of Childhood,* Goodman stresses the point that there are remarkably few universals or exceptionless "laws" in the processes of child-rearing and child socialization. She writes: "The anthropological record speaks eloquently on this point, and makes clear that an enormous range of variation exists and is tolerable. . . . We must stop assuming that what we see, or think we see, in the children of our society at this time necessarily tells us what is universal or inevitable."[7]

She supports her point by citing an example from traditional Greek folk culture. In the villages teachers, parents, and other family members will deliberately tease, frighten, and lie to young children. The reason for this vicious treatment is that the children are being prepared for the kind of adult social world in which they will have to function. This is the way the children learn how to respond to taunts and lies without psychological damage. In the United States parents, carefully tutored by *Dr. Spock's Baby Book,* would consider such childrearing practices horrendous and certain to lead to the creation of a generation of neurotics!

Another example of what would be considered unthinkable in American educational philosophy produced some of the greatest scholars, intellectuals, and scientists the world has ever known. These are the schools of the "shetl" culture of Eastern Europe at the turn of the Twentieth century.

6. Ibid., p. 177.
7. Mary Ellen Goodman, *The Culture of Childhood,* p. 157.

Scholar after scholar who fled the pogroms and anti-Semitism of the European "shetls" or ghettos, described his early education in the "cheder" school as an experience where the teacher rapped his knuckles or beat his body over and over until he committed to memory every page of the Talmud, the Holy Book. These scorned and heinous methods of teaching, highly derogated and disparaged in American colleges of education, managed to light life-long fires for knowledge and learning in minds of numerous children rather than turning them against formal education. Why did this happen? It seems an unfathomable paradox when considered in the perspective of American educational philosophy and training. However, when one brings Goodman's thesis of a cross-cultural perspective in child socialization to bear on the "forced" memorization of the shetl school or the cruel teasing of Greek village children, the actions become understandable. The children in these situations are learning the rules of the game. They are learning how to play their society's games and to succeed. Further, they learn that the adults in the situation mean them no harm but are trying to prepare them for the difficulties of life. "We grossly underestimate their sensibilities if we assume that children are unable to identify affection and guidance, however bizarre (from our point of view) its cultural packaging. They can and do."[8]

What do seem to stand forth as cultural universals in the socialization of the young child are the expressions of affection and the need for guidance from the adult. These two actions are often intertwined. As we have seen in the two examples provided, the guidance, which includes training and teaching, might be meted out with severe discipline but the underlying expression of affectionate concern is implicit and communicated to the child.

It is in this light that teachers in the type of traditional early childhood program that stresses a Rousseauian child's garden, laissez-faire, "let the child just play" philosophy can be criticized. Here we have affection displayed, possibly, but little guidance, training, or teaching provided. Our lesson from the cross-cultural perspective strongly indicates that affection, love, and warmth for the young child is not enough. Adult guidance in the ways of the society must be provided early in life, as well.

THE IMPORTANCE OF PLAY ON CHILD SOCIALIZATION

Echoing the theme of chapter 2, the dramaturgic approach to education, the school setting, and the classroom social atmosphere, we can examine young children's play and children's games as performances imitating adult roles and situations. The toddler of two or three years

---

8. Ibid., p. 158.

emerges from solitary and parallel play patterns into the stage of cooperative or collective play at about four years of age. From this time to about
seven years of age children engage in forms of play characterized by this
imitation of adult occupations and pastimes. In American and Western
European culture this is usually playing "house," "store," "school," and
more recently "babysitter."

In a trenchant, extensive and outstanding collection of readings entitled,
Child's Play, R. E. Herron and Brian Sutton-Smith bring together a vast
store of scholarly research and analysis on children's play and games from
the biological, ecological, psychological, sociological, and anthropological
literature. In this volume Brian Sutton-Smith, a child psychologist from
New Zealand who has specialized in the study of children's games, develops
a theory of the role relationships and dynamics inherent in children's play
and games. He sees young children's play in reciprocal relationships between the actors and counteractors. Sutton-Smith describes various early
childhood singing games such as "Ring Around the Roses," "Luby Loo,"
"Farmer in the Dell," "In and Out the Window" as dramatizations or
performances, sometimes pantomimed, around a central character or
characters and a group of chorus response.

> In addition to these singing games for the four- to seven-year age
> group, there were also dialogue dramas featuring two central actors and
> a group—usually a witch, a mother and her children, with traditional
> dialogue spoken by the various characters. In general, the children were
> naughty, the witch stole them, and the mother retrieved them. The role
> organization of the singing games were collaborative and ritualistic.
> Thus "Punchinello" (a singing game of Italian origin) goes through a
> sequence of actions in the middle of the ring and is imitated by the chorus
> circling around him. The Punchinello is actor and the others are counter-
> actors.[9]

A lilting and spritely melody accompanies the words to "Punchinello":

Ho, there you are Puchinello
    Funny fellow!
Ho, there you are Puchinello,
    Funny do.
What can you do, Punchinello,
    Funny fellow!
What can you do, Puchinello
    Funny do.

(This is just one version of the song. Many folk songs and children's songs
have a number of renderings).

---

9. Brian Sutton-Smith, "A Syntax for Play and Games" in *Child's Play,* edited by
R. E. Herron and Brian Sutton-Smith (New York: John Wiley & Sons, Inc., 1971),
p. 302.

The Puchinello then proceeds to create a motion, action, or expression for the group to follow. Puchinello is in the center of the circle of children. The children respond by copying the motion.

The third verse of Punchinello continues:

Choose someone new, Puchinello
  Funny fellow.
Choose someone new, Puchinello
  Funny do.

And the singing game proceeds with a new Puchinello.

What is the fascination of this singing game for young children? What is the fascination and attraction of the myriad of singing games, dramas, dialogue, or circle games young children ask to pay over and over in the nursery school, kindergarten, or other early childhood settings?

The literature on child socialization suggests that these early childhood games and forms of play afford the child an opportunity to try on or to imitate the adult roles of the society. In Puchinello the child can be the parent or the teacher telling or rather showing the other children just what to do. There is social power that brings excitement and pleasure when one controls a group of others and can elicit a specific response from them. The child suddenly has a mastery over his peers and his social surroundings when playing these traditional children's games. The rules must be strictly adhered to. One must pick a "farmer" first in the "Farmer in the Dell"; a wife, second; then the dog; then the cat. If one attempts to change the order and pick a cat right after the farmer is chosen, a chorus of objections greet the innovator, especially in a kindergarten or first-grade class.

This behavior on the part of four- to seven-year-olds when playing games is highly consistent with Piagetian theory on the development of moral values and ethics in young children. Piaget wrote that in early childhood at the preoperational level, children held adamantly to the rules of the game.[10] Not one type of variation or change was allowed. The rules of the game were inviolate.

Piagetian theory also stresses the acquisition of the mental operation of reversibility, being able to go back to the original state at the start of the operation, seeing the transformation or changes that occurred as being reversible. Children functioning in the beginning phases of the pre-operational stage have not yet acquired reversibility. Sutton-Smith points out that these early childhood games pave the way for the child to develop reversibility in his thinking or mental operations in Piagetian terms.

10. *The Moral Judgment of the Child* (Glencoe, Ill.: The Free Press, Inc., 1948, originally published in 1932).

Particularly in games where the roles of various characters, or the leader and the chorus are interchanged, the child can act out role reversibility.[11]

So we see that social scientists from a range of disciplines— psychology, sociology, anthropology, linguistics—utilize children's play and game as the basis for important theories, concepts, and research in socialization and enculturation. We learn to become human, members of a family group, a community, a culture, or society through the games we play as little children.

WHERE STEREOTYPING IS RAMPANT — BOOKS FOR YOUNG CHILDREN

Educators and lay people alike will readily admit that probably the most important and influential educational materials in the young child's classroom are first readers, those picture books, storybooks, work books and primers with which the child learns to read. After all, literacy is the key to modern, technological American culture. The school's most important task is to teach the child to read. Now the content, substance, format, even the illustrations in books for young children have suddenly come under fire and withering criticism from almost every interest group, ethnic subculture, minority affiliation, and, most recently, from women, a majority (51 percent) in America!

The campaign for publishers to provide more meaningful, realistic, and honest views of inner-city and family life for beginning readers in the public schools of America has been waged since the 1950s. Joining the movement in the past two decades have been educators and writers representing the minority groups, first blacks, then Hispano and Indian elements of American society. Rural and suburban groups have plied their pressures. Most recently it has been women's organizations that have entered the fray with a range of ammunition including a bibliography of appropriate non-sexist children's books titled, "Little Miss Muffet Fights Back!"

Historical Views Mirror Social Attitudes. Taking an historical approach to viewing the impact of the child's first readers on socialization and enculturation (internalizing the values of the society) clearly reveals the extreme bias, rigidity, and stereotyping reflected in children's books since public education began in America. Two interesting and scholarly studies particularly will be reviewed here to underscore this assertion. A unique approach to the problem was developed by Richard Mandel of the University of Chicago. In his article, "Children's Books: Mirrors of Social Development," he discusses his study that examined two sets of children's

---

11. Ibid., p. 303.

beginning readers from two periods of United States history. One from mid-nineteenth century, the Rollo series by Jacob Abbott published from 1844 to 1860, and one from the mid-twentieth century, the Dick and Jane series published by Scott, Foresman, and Company, during the 1950s.

The Rollo series of the nineteenth century strongly exemplifies the moral code, values, and attitudes of the period. America was mainly a rural society then, so the stories are set on a farm. The content stresses the fact that the world is a serious place fraught with sources of trouble. "Even more important, however, is a feeling that while Rollo is potentially a good boy, he is filled with bad impulses and tendencies that he must be constantly on the watch for and that he must learn to suppress."[12]

Also, Rollo's father is the most important person in his life. It is the father who presents the problem to be solved or the goal to be reached. Father is the purveyor of wisdom, the doler-out of punishment, the corrector, and the rewarder. Father is all-powerful in the Rollo series.

In direct contrast, Mandel notes that the Dick and Jane books consist almost entirely of children's conversations. Where adults do appear they are usually reacting to situations established by the children.

> The children spend their time having *fun* while playing with one another, while going to school, or while participating in humourous little incidents described as *funny* or *silly*. An unbelievable amount of time is spent at parties they host for one another and in planning and attending social events, usually birthday parties at which gifts are given. The children frequently visit relatives and neighbors and go in groups to places like zoos and construction sites.[13]

Mandel concludes that children's books reflect the wishes of the wider society for the type of life it desires for its youth. He feels that investigating children's literature is a valuable source for obtaining information on the customs, attitudes, and ethics of a society.

Further, one cannot help note that Rollo series mirrors an American society characteristic of Riesman's category of the innerdirected man, while the Dick and Jane series is characteristic of the other-directed man in the Riesman typology. (See David Riesman, Nathan Glaser, and Reuel Denney, *The Lonely Crowd.*)

Now let us examine a study that investigated primary readers in the United States from 1600 to 1966. Professor Sara Zimet of the University of Colorado developed a coding manual for rating sex role behavior of adult and child story characters in primary reading texts. Each story in a primary reading text from six time periods beginning with Period I, in

---

12. Richard I. Mandel, "Children's Books: Mirrors of Social Development, *Elementary School Journal,* 64 (January, 1964): 193.
13. Ibid., p. 197.

1600–1776, through Period VI, 1940–66, was rated on the following dimensions:

1. *Characters*—categories such as "children only," "children and mother," "adults only," "animals only" were used.
2. *Theme*—categories here included "active play," "pets," "lessons from life," "work projects."
3. *Age and Sex*—of the activities presented in the story.
4. *Role of the Adult*—i.e., "protector," "nurturer," etc.
5. *Outcome*—success, failure, uncertain.

Other aspects of the stories that were also rated included dependency behavior, aggressive behavior, environmental setting, occupations or work roles, and illustrations in the text.[14]

The findings present some interesting commentary on American attitudes and values: dependency behavior of children was consistently sustained throughout the six periods; from 1921-66 no clearly defined adult male and female behavior was portrayed, rather a child-centered adult model was featured functioning in a close-knit nuclear family; it was quite apparent that only one socioeconomic and cultural group was represented in the *total sample of texts* examined. (emphasis this author's)[15]

Zimet concludes with the following recommendations:

> The results of this study point to the need for a more pluralistic depiction of American life in reading textbooks. . . . It may very well be that the degree of success these texts achieve in teaching reading to children may depend upon their success as a socializing agent. Once we gain more insight, and understanding in the area, it may be possible to combine our knowledge of child development with the talent of the artist and write textbooks that are equally effective as instruments of acculturation and of teaching reading skill.[16]

Here Zimet is reinforcing Lippitt's thesis that the agents of socialization among the child's first readers are powerful forces which up to now have either echoed the viciousness that is the subtle heritage of American stereotypical behavior or presented a bland, colorless view of life to young children. This excellent opportunity to enculturate and socialize the child with open attitudes and values consistent with a pluralistic society is overlooked by the educational enterprise. Children are taught to read with the use of materials lacking depth in every dimension and truly worthy of the disparaging labels heaped upon primary readers by educators and laymen alike.

---

14. Sara Goodman Zimet, "Little Boy Lost," *The Record* (Teachers College Press, Columbia) 22 (Sept., 1970): 36–37.
15. Ibid., p. 39.
16. Ibid., p. 40.

Social Conflict is Eliminated. One of the most forthright and out-spoken attacks on elementary school instructional materials in general has been leveled by Jean Grambs in the volume, *Black Image; Education Copes with Color.* In describing the illustrations in children's readers (including social studies, spelling, and arithmetic books), Grambs notes that until recently these illustrations were almost exclusively of white-skinned children, parents, and their pets. (Spot manages to be white and black.) "No dark-skinned person intruded upon these pages unless he was a foreigner or in his own foreign country."[17]

Now publishers of elementary school texts have attempted to offer integrated textbooks with illustrations more characteristic of a multiethnic society. Yet Grambs writes that the themes of the stories have not changed. They still utilize the inane, trivial, "life is all fun" approach noted by Mandel earlier in this chapter. Grambs also points out that the elementary child has long been considered a delicate and sensitive creature who needs to be shielded from the realities of American life.

> This "new Dick and Jane" are not really very new. . . . The stories always end on an upbeat, there are no tears wept in anger or fear or despair; there are no pangs of hunger or vicious envy; the inventive nastiness of children is never even hinted at. That illness, death, divorce and crime abound in the world of the city and the worlds of the suburb and the farm is a fact of human experience still noticeably absent from textbook life.[18]

On the one hand we hear the continually voiced criticism of the super-ficiality of children's literature, criticism of that funny, silly undercurrent that characterizes children's story themes. Yet much scholarly research has ascertained the crucial nature of play and games in the socialization of the child. How do we reconcile what seem to be two antithetical positions? The answer is that the two positions do not relate to the same set of situations.

If stories for young children focused upon what theoretical objectives undergirded children's games and play rather than stressed the fun and momentary pleasure of the "play," such as receiving a new toy or the reward of getting to eat a cookie, the story themes would then be accep-table as socializing agents for our pluralistic society. If the stories indicated how Dick or Jane could first play one role, then another, hence learning to empathize with other ways of life, this approach would be most useful. But do the stories ever attempt such an approach?

---

17. Jean D. Grambs, "Dick and Jane Go Slumming: Instructional Materials for the Inner City Negro Child," in *Black Image: Education Copes with Color*, eds. J. D. Grambs and J. Carr (Dubuque, Ia.: Wm. C. Brown Co., Publishers, 1972), p. 59.
18. Ibid., p. 76.

The prospect of children's readers discussing problems or social conflict seems unlikely at this point in American educational practice. Yet we have pointed out that early childhood is the time of crucial intellectual and cognitive development, that young children are capable of far more understanding and a much greater range of empathetic feelings than adults give them credit for. Is the educational enterprise passing by superlative and optimum possibilities for socializing and enculturating the children of our society into the complex world of modern, technologized culture?

A LOOK AT MULTI-ETHNIC PICTURE BOOKS

How well are we fulfilling our obligations to the young children in our pluralistic society? A teacher of young children, also the mother of a three-year-old, was highly motivated to survey the libraries and bookstores of her area—a large city in the American Southwest where Chicano, Indian, and black minority groups are well represented—for early childhood books featuring minority group children as the central focus of the story and the illustrations. She investigated only those books published since 1967. Her investigations resulted in the following comments:

> The most disheartening group of books I surveyed were the books that featured American Indian children. Although it is estimated that 55-65 percent of American Indian population now lives in towns and cities and, further, that thousands and thousands of Indian children are attending boarding schools, I could not find one book that placed the Indian child in these contemporary settings. It seemed to me that books about Indian children were written for the consumption of white children. The stories were stereotyped and traditional, describing the Indian child on the reservation functioning in a tribal life style.
>
> In looking for meaningful books about Mexican-American (Chicano or Hispano) children a few were available but most left much to be desired. It was in the category of books for and about young black Americans that I found the most relevant, honest, and realistic portrayals. Many of these new children's books are written by black authors and published by black-owned businesses. Hopefully in the near future we will see the same situation in terms of authors and publishing companies among Indians and Mexican-Americans.[19]

SOME EXAMPLES — ANNOTATED BIBLIOGRAPHY

Indian Children

Friskey, Margaret. *Indian Two Feet and His Eagle Feather*. Chicago: Children's Press, 1967. Illustrated by John and Lucy Hawkinson.

The story of an Indian boy who tries to show his bravery by saving his village from a flood when the men are away hunting. This book

19. Ann Kaslow (unpublished paper for Educational Sociology, Graduate Level, School of Education, University of Denver, December, 1971).

Fig. 3.2. Anglo child's self-portrait.

Fig. 3.3. Anglo child's self-portrait.

Fig. 3.4. Anglo children's self-portrait.

Fig. 3.5. Black child's self-portrait.

Fig. 3.7. Black child's self-portrait.

Fig. 3.6. Black child's self-portrait.

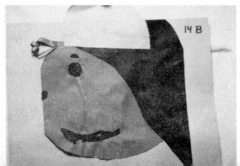

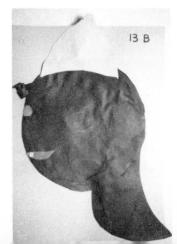

Fig. 3.8. Chicano child's self-portrait.

Fig. 3.9. Chicano child's self-portrait.

Fig. 3.10. Chicano child's self-portrait.

These self-portraits and those in figs. 3.2-3.7 were created by second-graders from three different schools representing three different ethnic backgrounds—Anglo, Black, and Chicano. The design for the research study was developed by Richard Dovenberg while at the University of Denver. It called for the children to use any *kind* of construction paper they chose from a variety of materials placed before them and to create a picture of themselves. The "rules" of this "game" included the directions that only scissors, paste, and construction paper could be used to create the self-portraits, no crayon or pencils. (The background paper was a pale green or other neutral color.) Notice the size of figures, or of face and head only. This type of project can be very revealing and informative to the sensitive teacher seeking insights to and greater understanding of the children being taught.

presents a picture of traditional Indian society but does include one element of positive self-image for the young Indian. Indian-Two-Feet says over and over again, "I'm an IN-DI-AN, IN-DI-AN, An, IN-DI-AN, Proud-of-it, Proud-of-it."

Henck, Sigrid. *Buffalo Man and Golden Eagle.* New York: McCall Publishing Co., 1970. Illustrated by the author.

Although Buffalo man lived alone, his life style is characteristic of the traditional Indian stereotype. The illustrations picture Buffalo Man with bright orange skin.

Mexican-American Children

Boloprese, Don. *A New Day.* New York: Delacorte Press, 1970. Illustrated by the author.

This author has taken the biblical theme of the birth of Christ and transposed it into modern Mexican-American terms. Jose and Maria are migrant workers and their baby is born in accommodations provided for them by a gasoline station owner. A realistic and contemporary story.

Bulla, Clyde. *Benito.* New York: Thomas V. Crowell Co., 1969. Illustrated by Valenti Angelo.

This book takes place in Southern California and is the story of a boy who, due to misfortune in his immediate family, goes to live with his uncle and aunt on their farm. Benito's love is art, which is looked upon with dismay by his relatives. He pursues his art work despite his uncle's attempts to stop him.

Serfozo, Mary. *Welcome Roberto!* New York: Follett Publishing Co., 1969. Photographs by John Serfozo.

The story deals with Roberto's experiences in a Head Start nursery school. We see him painting, singing, listening to records, building with blocks, playing with trucks, learning how to use the telephone and to tell time. Each page has the story line in both English and Spanish.

Black-American Children

Baker, Bette F. *What is Black?* New York: Franklin Watts, Inc., 1969. Photographs by Perry Willis II.

A beautiful book which employs impressions, ideas and photographs for instilling positive connotations for black awareness.

Hall, Elizabeth. *Evan's Corner.* New York: Holt, Rinehart & Winston, Inc., 1966, Illustrated by Nancy Grossman.

The story of an inner-city boy who lives with his family of eight in two rooms. He wants some place of his own and his understanding mother gives him a corner of a room. He makes it into someplace very special.

Keats, Ezra Jack. *Goggles!* Toronto: Macmillan Co., 1969. Illustrated by the author.

This is the story of a young boy, Peter, and how he, through his ingenuity, rescues a pair of goggles he has found in a vacant lot from three bullies.

Lexau, Joan. *Benjie on His Own.* New York: Dial Press, 1970. Illustrated by Don Boloprese.

The story of a fearful young boy who, because of his grandmother's sudden illness, is thrust into harsh reality and responsibility. He develops self reliance in facing and handling the consequences of his grandmother's illness. Very sensitively written.

McGovern, Ann. *Black Is Beautiful.* New York: Four Winds Press, 1969. Photographs by Hope Wurmfeld.

The book contains beautiful photographs of black "subject matter" with lovely, poetic text.

Rosenbaum, Eileen. *Ronnie.* New York: Parents' Magazine Press, 1969. Photographs by Gloria Lindauer and Carmel Roth.

Centers around the experiences of a boy of seven and his anticipation of a surprise his parents have for him. Deals with several emotions and with family relationships in a realistic and forthright manner.

Scott, Ann Herbert. *Sam.* New York: McGraw Hill Book Co., 1967. Illustrated by Symeon Shimin.

The story of how Sam, the youngest child in his family, feels when everyone is too busy to pay attention to him. Ends on a happy note.

Steptoe, John. *Stevie.* New York: Harper and Row, 1969. Illustrated by the author.

Written in ghetto dialect. Stevie comes to stay with Robert and his family (Robert's mother babysits). Robert resents the imposition. However, when Stevie finally leaves several months later, Robert realizes that Stevie wasn't so bad after all.

Steptoe, John. *Uptown.* New York: Harper and Row, 1970. Illustrated by the author.

This book takes the form of a conversation between two boys about the things they have done together and what they want to be. Their conversation touches upon junkies, Black Power, the army, the police, hippies, Karate and a black book store. Written in heavy dialect speech ("my main man"), it is a unique children's book.

Udry, Janice. *What Mary Jo Shared.* Chicago: Albert Whitman and Co., 1966. Illustrated by Eleanor Mills.

A sensitive portrayal of a shy little girl who can't think of anything to "share" (show and tell) with her class. Finally, she does think of something very special to share—her father. Her novel presentation is a great success.

Yezback, Steven. *Pumpkinseeds*. New York: Bobbs Merrill Co., Inc., 1969. Illustrated by Mozelle Thompson.

A young boy is given a nickel by his mother to purchase a treat. He buys some pumpkin seeds and after several negative encounters with people with whom he tries to share them, he happily shares them with some pigeons.[20]

An Effort at Pluralistic Representations. It is relatively easy to criticize elementary school instructional materials that are already on the market and being used with young children. However, it requires much knowledge, expertise, background, and an understanding of child growth and development to create worthwhile and appropriate curriculum materials for early childhood. A world-renowned social scientist was heard to remark, "If you can't teach it to the second grade, you do not know it!" Can we find any material of such stature available for young children at this time? This writer thinks such materials are just now coming from publishing houses that recognize the need for a totally new approach to learning for young children.

One example of the type of instructional material that recognizes the pluralistic nature of our country and a growing world society is *Social Studies Series: Focus on Active Learning* published by Macmillan, with senior authors John Jarolimek and Bertha Davis. The first book of the series is titled *You and Me* and was written by Charlotte Zolotow and illustrated by Robert Quackenbush. This social studies series features much more than a set of text books; it is truly multi-media material, with accompanying maps, study and demonstration prints, records, films, and excellent teacher guides.

It is in the children's book, *You and Me*, that one finds a sincere attempt to bring to young children an understanding of the universals, yet with variations, that the patterns of human life styles around the globe can take. Illustrated with rich, warm, colorful drawings, the story line begins with a generalized discussion of "Your Family." Part two then takes up, "Their Families"—city families, seaside families, farm families. The story reads:

---

20. For an extensive annotated bibliography on books for black-American children see Appendix 1, "Annotated Bibliography of Integrated and Black Books for Children," prepared by Barbara Glancy in *Black Image: Education Copes with Color*, edited by J. Grambs and J. Carr (Dubuque, Ia: Wm. C. Brown Co., Publishers, 1972), pp. 155-76. Another excellent publication that discusses many types of ethnic literature for children and adolescents is *Emerging Humanity: Multi-ethnic Literature for Children and Adolescents* by Ruth K. Carlson (Wm. C. Brown Co., 1972).

How can it be
that the boy in the farmhouse
lives
in so many ways
more like a French boy in the French countryside
than like boys
in cities,
in suburbs,
in seasides
        of America, his own country?
How can it be
that the boy who lives in the city
in an apartment house,
an American boy,
lives a life
more like a Dutch boy in the city of Amsterdam,
thousands of miles away,
than like boys
on farms,
in suburbs,
or seasides
        of America, his own country?
The place they live
decides a lot
about
the shape of their house,
the food they eat,
the things they see
each day.
It helps decide
the kind of work
their fathers do.
For you can't be a farmer
and grow vegetables in the city.
You can't be a fisherman
and catch fish
on a farm.
You can't be a city worker
and go to your job each day
all the way from the seashore.
So the farmer,
the fisherman,
the office worker,
who live
on farms,
or by the water,
or in cities
of America
are in many ways—
in small daily ways—

very like
the farmer,
the fisherman,
the office worker
in lands far away.
Our children—
fisherman,
farmer,
suburban
or city,
know the same language,
have the same President,
live by the same laws
and have the same flag
    as each other.
And for all the differences
in where they live
and how they live
each day,
being American
makes them in some ways
the same.
    The more we know
    the more we see
    about each kind
        of family.[21]

Here are some sophisticated concepts about socialization and linguistics. Concurrently, the teacher's guide stresses such concepts and ideas as:

All over the world children grow up in families;
identifying the essential nature of family functions;
there is a great variety among the world's families;
identifying varied role allocations in families;
how do the physical settings of family life differ?
introducing the relationship between places and ways of living;
clarifying the uniquely human relationship between human beings and natural surroundings;
the family is the basic agency of socialization.

This is elementary school instructional material that recognizes the capacities of young children for inquiry, intellectual curiosity, and in-depth investigation into basic sociological theory at very early age levels. Also, here is instructional material for elementary school teachers that dignifies the intellectual capacity and abilities of those who work with young children!

---

21. Charlotte Zolotow, *You and Me* (New York: Macmillan Co., 1972), pp. 64, 66, 68, 70, 74.

SEX ROLE SOCIALIZATION IN PICTURE BOOKS

We cannot leave a discussion of the impact of children's first readers upon socialization without further attention to their implications on sex role models, sex-typed behavior, and the charges of sexism. The term "sexism" refers to bias against women. Sexism is a new word derived from a take-off on "racism." It is evident from even a cursory review of children's literature that sexism is rampant in books for children and youth, from picture books to stories for adolescents.

An extensive study has found that little girls are often invisible in children's books. If they appear at all, they are insignificant, passive, and stereotyped. Lenore J. Weitzman, a Yale sociologist, and three of her students, Deborah Eisler, Elizabeth Hokada, and Catherine Ross, studied the best in picture books for young children, the winners of the Caldecott Medal, given by the Children's Service Committee of the American Library Association for the most distinguished picture book of the year.[22] Books on the list of Caldecott winners and runners-up are ordered by practically all children's libraries in the United States, often selling as many as 60,000 copies.

The researchers analyzed the contents of all the Caldecott winners from the inception of the award in 1938 through 1971. Then they focused on the 18 winners and runners-up for the past five years. Just to be sure these books were representative, they also studied Little Golden Books that have sold more than three million copies each. Little Golden Books are often sold in supermarkets and drugstores where the more expensive children's books cannot be purchased. Further, they studied winners of the Newberry Award given by the American Library Association for the best book for school-age children. The last type of book in this study was what is called the "prescribed behavior" or etiquette book. These are matched sets of books—one for boys, one for girls—with titles such as *The Very Little Boy* and *The Very Little Girl* (Doubleday, 1962); *What Boys Can Be* and *What Girls Can Be* (Hallmark Cards, Inc., not dated); *Mommies* and *Daddies* (Random House, 1960). Whereas other books only employ sex role prescriptions, these books are explicit about the proper behavior for boys and girls. They also portray adult models and advise children on future roles and occupations.

The study tabulated the distribution of illustrations in the picture books as probably the single best indicator of the importance of men and women in these books. Because women comprise 51 percent of the population, it

---

22. Lenore Weitzman, Deborah Eisler, Elizabeth Hokada, and Catherine Ross, "Sex Role Socialization in Picture Books for Pre-School Children" (unpublished paper read at the American Sociological Association National Meeting, September 2, 1971, Denver, Colo., subsequently published in the *American Journal of Sociology*, 77: 1125–50).

was assumed that they should be similarly represented in roughly half of the pictures. However, in the sample of 18 Caldecott winners and runners-up in the past five years, 261 pictures of males were found, compared to 23 pictures of females. This is a ratio of 11 pictures of males for every one picture of females. If animals are included with obvious sexual identities, the bias is even greater. The ratio of male to female animals is 95 to 1.

The Yale sociologists feel that children are bound to receive the impression that girls are not very important, because no one has bothered to write books about them. In the world of children's books, boys race, climb, hide, search and rescue people, the study states, while girls watch. If girls do anything else, they cook or serve the food. Little girls often wear frilly, starchy, pink dresses that are too pretty to muss up by riding a bike, playing ball, or going to the zoo. They also smile a lot, which teaches that women are meant to please, to make others smile and be happy.

The researchers state:

> The rigidity of sex role stereotypes are not harmful only to little girls. Little boys may feel equally constrained by the necessity to be fearless, brave and clever at all times. While girls are allowed a great deal of emotional expression, a boy who cries or expresses fear is unacceptable. Just as the only girls who are heroines in picture books have boys' names or are foreign princesses, the only boys who cry in picture books are animals—frogs, and toads and donkeys. The price of the standardization and rigidity of sex roles is paid for by children of both sexes. . . . Thus, rigid sex role definitions not only create anguish and unhappiness in our children, but they also hamper our children's fullest development.[23]

The researchers conclude that preschool children invest their intellects and imaginations in picture books at a time when they are forming their self-images and future expectations. Their study shows that the girls and women depicted in children's books are a dull and stereotyped lot. They note that little girls receive attention and praise for their attractiveness, while boys are admired for their achievements and cleverness. For girls, achievement is marriage and becoming a mother. Most of the women in picture books have status by virtue of their relationships to specific men—they are the wives of the kings, judges, adventurers and explorers, but they themselves are not the rulers, judges, adventurers and explorers.

> Through picture books, girls are taught to have low aspirations because there are so few opportunities portrayed as available to them. The world of picture books never tells little girls that as women they might find fulfillment outside of their homes or through intellectual pursuits. Their future occupational world is presented as consisting primarily of glamour

---

23. Ibid., p. 15.

and service. Women are excluded from the world of sports, politics, and science. They can achieve only by being attractive, congenial and serving others.[24]

It has been all too easy for teachers of young children not to "rock the boat," not to question the values and attitudes of the mass culture. If, through the years, women and girls have been discriminated against in children's literature, this has been accomplished with the uncontested support of the overwhelming number of female teachers who work with young children.

SES and Sex

The Yale study, as thorough and exhaustive as it is, with an adroit research design and carefully investigated data, overlooked an important sociological factor in the effects of children's books on child socialization and sex role stereotypes. The variable they ignored was socioeconomic status (SES) or the impact of social class upon sex-role stereotypes, sex-role behavior, and parental expectations for career development for sons versus daughters. Mainly, it is middle-class parents who buy books for their children. But it has been demonstrated by a number of studies that public schools serving middle-class children tend to have more materials and greater variety of materials than those schools serving lower-class or working-class populations. (See Patricia C. Sexton, *Education and Income* [New York: Viking Press, 1965].

On the other hand, there have been relatively few research studies that have formally investigated the impact of curriculum materials on sex-role stereotyping and more specifically on occupational aspirations of boys and girls at the elementary-school level. However, much emphasis in educational sociology and guidance and counseling has been placed on career development, experience in the world of work, and occupational choices at the high-school level. A classic and often cited study in this category was done by Joseph Kahl in the 1950s, "Educational and Occupational Aspirations of 'Common Man' Boys" (*Harvard Educational Review*, 23 [1953]: 186-203). We would stress that all this emphasis on career choices at the secondary-school level seems too late to overcome the bias and influences already inculcated in the child during his earlier socialization. This seems particularly to apply in the area of sex-role stereotyping and career choices.

To support this contention let us look at some of the attitudes expressed by high school career counselors, both men and women, from a recent survey done in the winter of 1971:

---

24. Ibid., p. 25.

Yes, I do remind girls that they may work part of their lives and should have a skill they can fall back on. I suggest that they take typing and shorthand, so that they will have a marketable skill.

These girls aren't interested in men's occupations. They never ask me for information about them. I certainly couldn't suggest that a girl go into the building trades. Why, I wouldn't want *my* daughter exposed to that rough language. (It was then suggested that he had better not send his daughter to college either if this really bothered him.)

I have a boy who is my counselee, and he is in electronics and can't find a job. I would feel very badly if there was a job opening and a girl was given that job instead of him.

Women work for the luxuries, so that they don't have to make much money. In fact, it's because they would work for so much less that teachers' salaries have traditionally been so low.

It's a man's world. There aren't enough jobs for everyone, so men ought to have the jobs — particularly the high paying jobs.

I have to be realistic in my counseling. I can't realistically tell a girl she should enter a man's profession. She might not get the job anyway after she was trained.[25]

One aspect that does seem evident, though, is that lower socioeconomic status children are required to adhere to more stereotyped sex roles and are more limited in their job choices as well. The wealthier one's family, the more options one has, even to the point of being highly deviant in occupational choices. In the consideration of the influence of socioeconomic status upon sex-role behavior and occupational aspirations, or SES↔SEX, one can predict changes will occur in the coming decades. As women's groups press for more open attitudes and a more equalitarian approach in sex-role socialization, young mothers and, it is to be hoped, teachers of young children will take up the cause. As a result, appropriate sex-role behavior and sex-linked career opportunities will undergo a redefinition. New alternatives and a wider variety of choices will be presented to youth in the future.

Men in Early Childhood — A New Alternative. One of these evolving alternatives in career choices that historically has been sex-linked is the teacher of young children. Traditionally the teacher in nursery schools and kindergartens has been a *woman*. In recent years, with the recognition of the crucial nature of early learning and intellectual development, more and more men have found their way into careers in working with young children. The long-range effects of males as role models of the teacher of young boys and girls is yet to be felt. Psychologists and psychiatrists have voiced enthusiastic support for this new alternative—shades of Freudian-

---

25. Linda Carroll, "The Making of a Woman" (unpublished paper, Educational Sociology, School of Education, University of Denver, December, 1971), p. 17.

ism! Following is a quotation from the term paper of a male student in an early childhood education course. This student is a member of the varsity basketball team at his university, a senior who elected the early childhood course as an optional educational experience. Part of the course requirements was to spend one or two sessions a week at a Head Start or other early childhood program as an aid or assistant in the classroom.

This secondary education major turned Head-Start assistant teacher writes:

> The personal experience and satisfaction that I gained through my work there [the Head Start Center] have been fantastic. At first, I must admit, I did not think I was going to like it. I felt very much out of place and the whole situation looked very negative. Needless to say, after a very short while my attitude changed completely. Working with the children gave me great pleasure and I found myself becoming very much involved with them.
>
> One thing that was quite noticeable was the lack of the male image for the children. At first they seemed hesitant and somewhat afraid to come to me. This problem could have been due to a number of things. For example, the lack of a father or a domineering father always yelling at home. Or perhaps being as big as I am (6 feet, 8 inches) my size might have scared them. Thus hesitancy on the children's part could have been due to any number of things. After becoming friends with all of the children there seemed to be an exact reverse of the previous situation. Instead of being hesitant they became overly anxious towards me, especially the boys. I feel that this situation again was due to the lack of a male image. After realizing that I was their friend, especially the boys, I was someone different that they could associate with. To the boys I was someone they could wrestle with, play football with, or play trucks with. In general, I was someone whom they could roughhouse with. To the girls I feel that I was something different in the way of a friend. I felt that most of the girls were never really close to any type of male figure and when I played with them and helped them in their work they seemed kind of awed at my presence. The associations made between the girls and myself became quite strong.
>
> After going through this experience at the Head Start Center, I can definitely see where there is a need for more men in the field of early childhood education. *Personally, I feel that every man should get the chance to work in some sort of early childhood education center* just so he could experience what the importance of the male image is to very young children [emphasis supplied].[26]

We visited this Head Start Center one very cold winter morning, and with delight and pride observed our student interacting with the four-year-olds he describes. A small table containing a variety of beans differing in size and colors with bowls, spoons, and sifters had been set out by the

---

26. Dick Scharphorn (term paper, Early Childhood Education, School of Education, University of Denver, December, 1971), pp. 2–3.

Fig. 3.11. "Mr. Greg, my teacher." (Courtesy Greg Marett.)

head teacher of the Center. Our student teacher had gathered five children around him. One little girl nestled between his legs as he sat on a stool next to the table filled with containers of beans. Two boys stood by his right side, while a boy and another girl clung to his left thigh and knee intent on what was about to happen with the beans.

Our student then asked one boy to hold a sifter (obtained from the sand and water play equipment) over a large bowl. He motioned and directed another boy to pick up a container of large brown beans and pour it into the sifter. "Watch and see how many beans come through," he remarked to the other three youngsters. All the children were intently involved. No beans came through the sifter. Then the request came to one of the girls. "Pick up that jar of small beige beans and let's pour it into the sifter. Watch now, what happens!"

To the children's delight, the smaller, beige-colored beans fell through the sifter into the bowl. They became excited. "What is happening?" our student asked. The children replied, "The beans, the beans, the beans came through!" "Yes," he clarified for them, using his knowledge of Piagetian theory obtained from the early childhood education course. "Some beans are too large to go through the seive. Those are the brown beans. Some beans are not so large. The beige beans are smaller, small enough to slip through the sieve and fall into the bowl. Now let us see what happens with those reddish beans. Do you think they will fall through the sifter?" And the children continued their lesson in observation, investigation, and classification with enthusiasm and much satisfaction.

Here we observe not only a creative application of Piagetian theory with a group of young children, but an exciting learning environment with an able, supportive male in the role of teacher of young children!

CHANGING SCENES: IS THE LITTLE CHILD REALLY LOST?

Young children are deeply conscious of the social arena in which they function. Although adults would characterize children as innocent and naive about social interactions, in actuality the young child learns to cope with his socializers in a number of ways, as Lippitt has pointed out. Further, we tend to think that what our children do are typical behavior patterns for young children the world over. Goodman has dramatically challenged this misconception with her anthropological approach. Stress has been placed on the crucial nature of games and play in child socialization in the school setting as well as informally. However, the agency of

Fig. 3.12. Black child's self-portrait. (Courtesy Richard Dovenberg.)

socialization that has been held up for examination as the most powerful force in child socialization are the picture books and first readers the child encounters. If we redefine social roles and social status in our rapidly changing culture, it is certain to have impacts and effects on the socialization of the young child in his classroom and in the broader society.

Sources

Boocock, Sarane S. *An Introduction to the Sociology of Learning.* Boston: Houghton Mifflin Co., 1972.

Carlson, Ruth. *Emerging Humanity: Multi-ethnic Literature for Children and Adolescents.* Dubuque: Wm. C. Brown, Co., Publishers, 1972.

Clausen, John, ed. *Socialization and Society.* Boston: Little, Brown and Co., 1968.

Elkin, Frederick and Handel, Gerald. *The Child and Society: The Process of Socialization,* 2nd ed. New York: Random House, 1972.

Goodman, Mary Ellen. *The Culture of Childhood.* New York: Teacher's College Press, 1970.

Grambs, Jean and Carr, John, eds. *Black Image: Education Copes with Color.* Dubuque, Ia.: Wm. C. Brown, Co., Publishers, 1972.

Herron, R. E. and Sutton-Smith, Brian. *Child's Play.* New York: John Wiley & Sons, Inc., 1971.

Howe, Florence. "Sex Stereotypes Start Early." *Saturday Review,* October 16, 1971.

Jarolimek, John and Davis, Bertha, eds. Teacher's Guides, *Social Studies Series: Focus on Active Learning.* New York: The Macmillan Co., 1971.

Lippitt, Ronald. "The Neglected Receiver: The Child" in *Social Science in the Schools: A Search for Rationale.* New York: Holt, Rinehart & Winston, Inc., 1971.

Mandel, Richard. "Children's Books: Mirrors of Social Development." *Elementary School Journal,* vol. 64 (January, 1964).

Piaget, Jean. *The Moral Judgment of the Child.* Glencoe, Ill.: Free Press, 1948.

Riesman, David, Glaser, Nathan, and Denney, Reuel. *The Lonely Crowd.* New Haven: Yale University Press, 1961.

Weitzman, Lenore; Eifler, Deborah; Hokada, Elizabeth; Ross, Catherine. "Sex Role Socialization in Picture Books." American Sociological Association, 1971. Subsequently published in the *American Journal of Sociology* 77: 1125–50.

Zimet, Sarah Goodman. "Little Boy Lost." *The Record,* Teachers College Press, 1970.

—————————, ed. *What Children Read In School.* New York: Grune and Stratton, 1972.

chapter 4

The Young Child
and Social Education
for a World Society

In the previous chapter references to customs and folkways of cultures, societies, and subgroups around the world were used to illustrate concepts and theories about the socialization of the young. It seems apparent that we can no longer contemplate the education of our children without a world perspective. Our present degree of expertise in technology along with an affluent life style that affords travel and social interchange for whole families, as well as for young single adults and business people, has made the possibility of world travel a reality even in the lives of young children. An influence of still greater impact is now on the horizon, one which may have vast implications for child socialization in the near future. This is the sweeping changes in monetary values and currency exchanges predicated on world trade that are occurring in the early 1970s. All too soon it will be the elementary school children of today who are grown up and manning the production lines and sitting at the drafting boards preparing products, goods, and services for a world market. How well will these workers in the coming years be able to adjust to a world of consumers with folkways and traditions that may differ greatly from their own? If American children are socialized with stereotypic images of "foreign" people, how well can they function in a world society?

In an earlier volume I urged the need for preparing our children, from the time they are born, to live in a pluralistic multicultural world. I wrote:

> Beyond developing within the child the general ability to perceive the world as a multi-nation whole, we must also develop what might be called "worldmindedness," or a sense of global responsibility. Children now need to become sensitive to the needs of others. They must understand the human condition not only intellectually, but emotionally as well. Children can be made to understand and appreciate the cultural diversities and the likenesses of the world of people that surround them. . . .

95

Being worldminded encompasses far more than merely bettering inter-group relations. Worldmindedness is based upon humanistic philosophy, grounded in the arts and humanities and the major contributions the social sciences bring to furthering knowledge about the human condition.[1]

Teachers of young children can dodge the issue and rationalize that teaching about a world perspective is appropriate for the later elementary school years, or possibly at second- or third-grade levels. "Four, five and six-year-olds just are not ready for that kind of learning experience," they may say. It seems redundant to continually state that early childhood educators have demonstrated the sensitivity and awareness of young children to their social scene. Therefore, the social education of the child in a world society and for a worldwide culture can begin in the early years. Stimulated by an advanced training workshop in leadership in early childhood education, held at the University of Denver, Summer, 1971, Carolyn Dungan, an experienced and worldminded kindergarten teacher herself, developed the following project:

ARTS AND HUMANITIES RESOURCES AND MATERIALS FOR DEVELOPING WORLDMINDEDNESS IN THE KINDERGARTEN

Introduction. Our school has a unique cultural, ethnic, and socio-economic diversity unlike any other school in the district. For example, the student body includes Negro, Caucasian, Chicano, Latin American, Eskimo, Hawaiian, and American Indian—Sioux, Hopi, Cherokee, and Zuni. In addition, students have come from the following countries: England, Scotland, Ireland, France, Germany, Czechoslovakia, Sweden, Norway, Spain, Italy, India, Turkey, Egypt, Korea, Japan, China, Australia, and Mexico.

Our school population is also the most transient in the district. In some classrooms, 100 percent turnover from September to June is not uncommon. In addition, family incomes range from the poverty level to affluency, so that the students live in new, modern, high-rise apartments; one-family residences; and crowded, low-rent units.

This wide variation in ethnic and cultural backgrounds of the school population, the mobility of the students, and the economic diversity dramatically illustrate the necessity for developing an awareness and understanding of a '"world citizenship" concept in young children. Only through cooperative efforts among people everywhere can we begin to solve the problems confronting the entire world—peace, racial equality, population control, and poverty, to mention only a few.

---

1. Edith W. King, *The World: Context for Teaching in the Elementary School* (Dubuque, Ia.: Wm. C. Brown Co., Publishers, 1971), pp. 3–4.

Fig. 4.1. Replication of the poster from *Discovering the World* multi-media materials. (Courtesy Spoken Arts, Inc., New Rochelle, and Phyllis Batty, kindergarten teacher.) Created by a kindergartner, Ashland Elementary School, Denver, Colorado.

Purpose.   If I understood, perhaps I'd see
              why some people live in ways that seem odd to me.[2]

It is hypothesized that experience with music, dance, literature, drama, games, art, history, and holidays and customs of other lands is an appropriate context for developing a sensitivity to and an awareness of the diversity and similarity of various cultures throughout the world. Therefore, the purpose of this project was to compile a list of resources and materials in the arts and humanities suitable for use with kindergarten children in both the cognitive and affective domains.

Discussion. Although the focus of this paper is on developing worldmindedness in kindergarten children at our inner-city school, materials included are appropriate for use with all children regardless of where they attend school. It has been suggested that in every school sociological and ethnic riches are present in the form of the traditions, artifacts, the material culture, the talents and the knowledge of the families whose children attend the schools. Through careful planning and sensitivity, the teacher can utilize these resources in the classroom in order to develop cross-cultural understandings.

With the diversity of cultural background present, the teachers at our school have available a unique variety of resources and an unusual opportunity for developing worldmindedness. The use of resource persons from the school community can be effectively supplemented by multimedia materials, literature, dramatic activities, music, dance, and art.

The lists of annotated materials (see Appendix A in this book) are by no means exhaustive, but rather examples of the types of materials available which are suitable for use with young children. The materials included were personally evaluated and judged to be appropriate for kindergarten children. It is hoped that the brief annotation will be helpful to teachers in selecting resources for a specific need. Each teacher is encouraged to locate additional resources to meet the needs of her specific school setting, using the cultural and ethnic backgrounds of her students as a point of departure.

It is particularly important to emphasize the need to familiarize the "underprivileged" children of suburbia, cited by Alice Miel, with the rich diversity of American life, the problems facing city children, and the inherent dignity of every human child.

From a four-year study of how suburban children are taught to live in a multicultural society, Miel summarizes her findings:

1. The suburban child is largely insulated from any contact with a life different from his own.
2. Suburban children learn to be hypocritical about differences at a very early age.

---

2. Charlotte Zolotow, *You and Me* (New York: The Macmillan Co., 1971), p. 62.

3. Group prejudices develop very early.
4. With few exceptions, economic inequality is ignored in suburbia.[3]

In addition, Miel states that the suburban child tends to be materialistic, self-centered, academically striving, conforming, and overly-concerned about cleanliness and order. These values appear to have a direct bearing on how suburban children feel about persons different from themselves. Implications for early education for responsible world citizenship before prejudices are internalized are clear.

Taylor writes that too often, teachers, parents, and students ". . . become so accustomed to their own school and their own community, with so little chance to become directly involved with schools and communities completely unlike their own, that they tend to assume that what happens in their own environment is what happens and should happen everywhere else."[4]

Teachers, then, need to broaden the horizons of young children in order to increase their sensitivity to others and to develop world-mindedness.

Children need help in learning to understand and respect people different from themselves. In order to develop positive social responsibility, it is necessary to focus on children's attitudes rather than merely subject matter. Therefore, it is essential to determine what children already know or believe in order to clarify confusions and build new learnings. In addition, children must be encouraged to acknowledge and objectively examine cultural differences and commonalities.

The role of the teacher as a model of desired behavior for young children cannot be over-emphasized. Bronfenbrenner states: ". . . the teacher must reflect not the preferences and prejudices of a particular class, but the interests of all segments of the society in their quest for a better world."[5]

Certainly, in order to conduct an effective program for young children, teachers must be committed to "worldmindedness" and the values of the world citizenship concept. Daily contact with a teacher sincerely committed to a world perspective and respect for the humanism and dignity of all men is a powerful force for developing worldmindedness in young children and socially responsible behavior in adults.

Although changing teacher attitudes is beyond the scope of this paper, the reader is referred to "An In-Service Program for Teachers"[6] for a list of appropriate resources for an in-service elementary-teacher training program. In addition, it is the responsibility of the teacher to

---

3. Alice Miel, *The Shortchanged Children of Suburbia: What the Schools Don't Teach About Human Differences and What Can Be Done About It* (New York: Institute of Human Relations Press, 1967), p. 13.
4. Harold Taylor, *The World as Teacher* (Garden City, N.Y.: Doubleday & Co., Inc., 1969), p. 39.
5. King, *The World*, p. 193.
6. Ibid., p. 143.

be as knowledgeable and informed as possible regarding the traditions, history, and meaning of group practices for all cultural groups presented to the children. Library research and home and community visitation are effective means of teacher education. Similarly, it is absolutely essential for meaningful education of young children that the teacher understand and be sensitive to the cultural traditions of each child in her classroom.

Miel recommends the following school practices as prerequisites to an understanding of and sensitivity to human differences.[7]

1. *Develop higher thought processes.* Children need experience in analyzing and evaluating controversial subjects.

2. *Foster understanding of the student's own community, its structure and operation.* Children need continuous help in building a realistic picture of their own community, including knowledge of the social problems existing within their community.

3. *Help children attain some insight into their own values and those of others.* Children need to understand the values which influence them, and to recognize that all people need not hold the same values.

4. *Develop an empathic understanding of others.* The classroom should be a laboratory for helping children learn to wark and live with others.

In planning activities for developing worldmindedness, emphasis should be on developing an appreciation for the humanism and dignity of mankind. In addition, teachers should understand that young children need to be actively involved in learning activities.

Music and dance are especially appropriate for developing warm feelings toward people of other cultures. Art experiences provide young children with an excellent media for expressing their feelings. In addition, music and art can help young children understand the interdependence of societies, and the contributions of countries around the world to our own culture.

Literature, dramatic activities, and role-playing experiences provide young children opportunities for verbal extension, and exploration of other cultures and values during the crucial years of intellectual, emotional, and attitudinal development. A study of cross-cultural holidays and festivals help children undertand the diversity throughout the world, and examine the values and customs of their own society. In addition, cross-cultural studies provide minority children with opportunities for pride in their heritage. Similarly, a study of the history of art work and cultural customs and traditions develops an appreciation for current modes of living.

As young children begin to understand and appreciate other cultures, they develop greater understanding and appreciation for their own culture. Fersh writes: "Ignorance about others perpetuates ignorance

---

7. Miel, *The Shortchanged Children*, p. 57.

about oneself, because it is only by comparisons that one can discover personal differences and similarities. The "glass" through which other cultures are viewed serves not only as a window; it serves also as a mirror in which each can see a reflection of his own way of life.[8]

Therefore, young children who feel good about themselves can be more accepting of children different from themselves. However, children must be given a realistic approach to the study of other cultures including the transitional phases of those cultures. For example, not only is it important to study the traditions and customs of a culture, but also it is essential to study how that same society is changing, and what it is attempting to achieve. In addition, kindergarten children should be given opportunities to evaluate other cultures as well as their own culture.

Culminating activities following cross-cultural studies might include exhibits of children's art work, singing, dancing, and dramatizations for parents, children in the local school, and children in other schools.

Summary. The need for developing worldmindedness and responsible world citizenship has been defined. Because the early years in a child's life are crucial for developing attitudes, beliefs, and values, the kindergarten classroom is an appropriate place for helping young children develop an understanding of and appreciation for cultural differences and commonalities.

With the diverse economic, cultural, and ethnic backgrounds of the kindergarten children at our school as a starting point, a list of annotated resources and materials in the arts and humanities suitable for use with kindergarten children was compiled. In addition, a theoretical framework for cross-cultural study with emphasis on the development of positive attitudes toward others was presented.[9]

A WORLD COMMUNITY OF EDUCATORS

As Dungan points out, the work of Alice Miel in investigating the "shortchanged children of suburbia" has been a source of inspiration and motivation for teachers of young children. More recently Miel has extended her concerns on intergroup relations to global perspectives and to the collaboration of educators all over the world. In a report of the World Conference on Education sponsored by the Association for Supervision and Curriculum Development at Asilomar, California, in 1970, Miel joins with Louise Berman to edit a volume on the addresses, reports and outcomes of the Conference.[10]

---

8. King, *The World,* p. 128.

9. Carolyn Dungan, "Arts and Humanities Resources and Materials for Developing Worldmindedness in the Kindergarten," mimeographed (Workshop: Leadership in Early Childhood Education, University of Denver, Summer, 1971).

10. Alice Miel and Louise Berman, *Educating the Young People of the World* (Washington, D.C.: Association for Supervision and Curriculum Development, 1970).

In pursuing the theme "Toward a World Community of Educators: Unity with Diversity" Miel notes that the word *world* was selected in preference to international since the focus is on the common responsibilities for the education of all the youth of the world. "The word *community* is employed in the sense of a group of people with joint character or likeness, in this case a common profession or calling, who are in communication with one another. . . . They are committed to a kind of expression which tries to transcend ethnocentric and egocentric barriers in genuine attempts to reach the mind and heart of another."[11]

Miel also points out that one of the functions of a world community of educators could be the study and exchange of variations in culture and education that might be useful in other settings. This is an exciting idea and the possibilities have hardly been tapped. We in America have just begun to recognize the successes of the British primary schools and the implications for teaching practices in our country. One of the outstanding resource persons at the ASCD World Conference on Education was the educational sociologist, Denis Lawton. Professor Lawton, a senior lecturer in curriculum studies at the Institute of Education, University of London, was the director of a three-year investigation into the social studies in British schools sponsored by the Schools Council.

Lawton believes that we can have education for social awareness and sociology can provide some of the necessary tools, such as the concepts of socialization, culture, and role. Sociology in the child's curriculum can offer a different way of looking at the world, a perspective which gives a new kind of social awareness. He has written that children in the primary schools are ready for such sociological investigations, in his estimation.[12]

HOW CHILDREN SEE SOCIETY

Why can we not utilize a world community of educators and a world filled with classrooms of children and teachers to develop exciting projects and programs in social education? Just as we exchange ideas and techniques at our local, regional, or national conferences and meetings, why cannot we obtain innovative and unique approaches from other countries, particularly English-speaking ones? Discussing these ideas with Professor Lawton in his office in the Institute of Education Building at the University of London one summer, we both agreed this certainly was possible. It was stimulating and comforting, too, to find someone else advocating the use of sociology in the

---

11. Alice Miel, "Toward a World Community of Educators: Unity with Diversity," in *Educating the Young People of the World* (Washington, D.C.: Association for Supervision and Curriculum Development, 1970), p. 83.
12. Denis Lawton, "Social Science in the Schools," *New Society*, April 25, 1968, p. 303.

curriculum of young children; someone else who felt that "children's social awareness was much more penetrating than adults give them credit for," as Lawton put it.

The educational sociologist described how the Schools Council, a powerful British educational organization composed of educators and lay people, held a conference at Warwick University in 1967. One of the topics discussed was the place of social studies in the curriculum of eight- to thirteen-year-old pupils, and it seemed to be generally agreed that the new knowledge included in the social sciences was often completely neglected by schools. There was some dispute about exactly what kind of social studies pupils of this age could be expected to understand, but it was felt that some effort should be made both to find out what some schools were already doing with some degree of success and also eventually to encourage other schools to take up promising practices. As a result, in September of 1968 a small team of two research officers, was appointed to survey and report on existing practice in schools, and to make a report to the Schools Council as to what additional materials might be helpful. Several of the projects reported by the investigation provide promising practices not only for British schools, but also for American schools. Keeping with Miel's suggestion of drawing from a world community of educators these projects in social studies from the report, Schools Council Working Paper No. 39, *Social Studies 8–13,* are presented here. Although these projects focus on children ages eight to eleven years of age, they involve younger children, five to seven years, in the activities and experiences.

PROJECT: BIRTH PLACES

This Oxfordshire school for juniors [ages 7+ to 11+] and infants [ages 5-7] is six years old, well appointed and equipped, and the "classrooms" are purpose built units, each one designed as a number of small differentiated working areas; most have a classroom library room or area with easy chairs, small coffee table, etc., an arts and crafts "messing about" area, and a couple of other areas for small group work. There are no corridors in the school, which allows extra space for the classrooms.

The 300 pupils at the school are largely drawn from the housing estates in which it stands, built to accommodate the labor demands from the town's two main factories. So the children are largely of working-class background. There are very few children of professional class parents, according to the head master [principal]. There are ten full-time teachers, thus average class size is 30 students per teacher. The school operates an integrated day, in that there is no timetabling by the headmaster. The concept behind this is that the teachers must start from the needs and/or interests of the individual pupil. This implies:

> that the teacher's job is to provide a "context" in which these needs and interests can be discovered and explored; and
> the organization of the school encourages the provision of such context.

The organization in the junior school is as follows:

> 7+-year-olds grouped with one teacher
> 8+-year-olds grouped with one teacher
> 9+–11+-year-olds grouped in three classes; the pupils remain with one teacher for two years.

It is claimed that this organization has the advantage of providing the child with stability, and of allowing as wide a variety of learning groups as is thought necessary at any given time.

The staff and pupils at the school enjoy a very friendly and informal relationship, and the activities of the children in and out of the working areas are very much "self-regulatory." For this reason it was an easy school to visit, since we could discuss ideas with teachers without interfering with children's learning.

This project was a survey of the birth-places of all the families whose children are pupils at the school. This was being done by a small group of children in one of the vertically grouped classes.

The idea was developed by the headmaster, after it arose out of a BBC program on primary school mathematics. The children wanted to do a survey, but did not know what subject to use. The headmaster suggested the following, which he said would be both original and useful to him, besides providing the pupils with an insight into one aspect of their neighborhood. The children might find out, record, and chart, the birth places of the children at the school and their parents' birth places as well. The class was enthusiastic about this idea and six children started the project.

They decided that the easiest way would be to go to each class and ask the pupils in it for the information they wanted. However, it soon became clear to them that this was time-consuming and inefficient as many children did not know where their parents had been born. So they discussed it with their form teacher who suggested that a questionnaire approach might be more successful. They drew up the questionnaire and sent it to parents with an explanatory letter from the headmaster. The rate of response was excellent, 195 returns out of 209 or 90 percent. The data gathered were then collated by the six children.

Two boys extracted the birth places of all the fathers, drew up a histogram, worked out percentages, and wrote up a report indicating the major findings. Two girls then took the questionnaires and did the same thing for the mothers. Then two other girls did it for children of the families. There was a concluding session in which the class looked at the findings, were encouraged to make comparisons and try to interpret the data.

The project therefore stimulated, as it was designed to do, some simple statistical work, some computation—the children learned how to do long division and had to decide on the most appropriate methods of presenting their data. In these terms alone, the class teacher thought the project had justified itself.

If it had remained as simply a technical exercise in some of the skills of numeracy, it would not have been of such interest to us in the area of social education. However, there was more to it than that. Firstly, the children had learned the valuable lesson that some ways of gathering information about society are more appropriate, and more reliable than others. They were able to appreciate that their initial attempts at investigation—by asking fellow pupils—were both inefficient and unreliable; and had come to realize that, for this project, a direct questionnaire could be much more useful. In interviews with us, the pupils could explain this lucidly and seemed clearly to have learned from their experience.

Secondly, the pupils had been encouraged not only to present their findings to the class, but also to attempt interpretations of their figures. Their major finding was that although nearly all the pupils were born locally, relatively few of their parents were. The most common birth place for non-local parents was London. In attempting to interpret this the pupils had to move from their figures to a consideration of the demands of local employment, and to the idea of "job mobility." This is a rather complex idea for young children to grasp, but is an important characteristic of modern industrial society. Our interviews suggest that the pupils involved had understood the following ideas.

1. Families in a small town nowadays will be from geographically varied backgrounds.

2. People move out from large urban areas primarily for "better" jobs.

3. When new industry moves into an area, a consequence of this move is the large-scale provision of suitable housing.

4. The labor market in a small town is more stable than in a large urban area.

5. In a small town with only two major industries, the acquisition of housing is closely related to occupations within those industries.

The research team went on to enlarge the possibilities of this project on birth places. This extension gives even wider possibilities for use by American classroom groups.

Had it seemed appropriate to the school to do so, the project could have been developed into a larger scale study of the phenomenon of "overspill." This could have taken many different approaches, but among the important ideas that teachers could encourage is a project of this sort, the following are important:

1. The attitudes of different groups in the town—the attitudes of locals to the newcomers. The children could interview and tape-record a sample of residents, to include newcomers and locals, and gain an impressionistic and vivid picture of their opinions on the town, their work, and the way their lives had been changed by the growth of the town.

2. An historical investigation from local records of the growth of housing and employment in the area. Apart from its intrinsic value, this could create opportunities for map work, model making, display work of all kinds, including sketching, painting and photography.

3. A study of the growth of income and expenditure through local rates and taxes.

4. A study of the growth in provision of local services and trade; transportation, education, welfare, shops and markets, etc.

Such a framework would allow the teacher to introduce general sociological and economics ideas: social change in a town; reference groups in a community; supply and demand; division of labor. Not that they need be presented as such. The pupils could be led to a consideration of such ideas after their observation and investigation of concrete phenomena—the residents, public records, local photographs, and press reports, visits, etc. But it is useful for teachers supervising a local project much as this to have generalizations from the social sciences in their minds, and in drawing together the children's work they could encourage them to interpret their findings by reference to such generalizations. By so doing, they will be helping to lay a foundation that will enrich pupils' approach to social studies at a later stage.[13]

PROJECT: LITTER

The school where this project was carried out is a co-educational junior and infants school with about 400 pupils and 12 full-time staff including the headmistress. The classes are operated mainly on an integrated day. The junior section here consists of one clas of 7+ age group; and two each of 8+, 9+ and 10+ age group but there is some vertical grouping and overlapping of age groups in the first school described. The

---

13. Denis Lawton, R. J. Campbell & Valerie Burkitt. Report to the Schools Council—Subsequently published as Schools Council Working Paper Number 39, *Social Studies 8–13* (London: Evans, Methuen Educational, 1971 and distributed in the United States by Citation Press), p. 7, 76–79.

buildings are seven years old and fairly modern but designed with the four-walled classroom as the basic unit. The school population is drawn from an area where there is a small village between two large urban centers. The social backgrounds of the pupils are comprised roughly of half affluent middle-class commuters, professional people, living in private homes, and half working-class people from the local authority housing project or estate, [as the British call them.]

This project developed from an unlikely situation. One of the teachers complained to three girls, whose job it was to sell crisps and nuts at breaktime, that there was far too much litter around the school. They were able to show that the make of the crisp bags that had caused the complaint, was not the make they sold, and the matter could have rested there. However, they decided to take things further and carried out a full-scale collection, weighing and classifying the litter.

Surprised by the amount of litter, they launched what turned out to be a social experiment. This experiment was basically a matter of taking six litter counts, with the three pupils altering the conditions likely to affect the amount of litter.

First Count—A straight-forward count of the pieces of litter; the playground was divided into areas near each classroom and the litter classified in these areas, and represented on a graph. This provided the baseline count of "normal" litter in the school.

Second Count—The teaching staff was asked to ignore all litter for a few days and then a further count was taken. The resulting graph represented a steep increase in litter in all classroom areas.

Third Count—A campaign of exhortation by the children was launched. In morning assembly and in individual school rooms, all children were appealed to, that they should make a positive attempt to reduce the amount of litter in the school. Then the count showed a dramatic reduction, and the litter fell below that recorded at the first count.

Fourth Count—The three girls produced posters, displayed them around the school and then took a fourth count. Their graph revealed a further drop in the junior classroom areas but not in the infant school areas, the five- and six-year-olds. They concluded that the poster campaign had not influenced the younger children either because many of them couldn't read the posters, or because they had *displayed the posters too high on the school walls* and notice boards for them to be noticed by the five and six-year-olds (emphasis supplied).

Fifth Count—The girls then aimed their propaganda at the infants. They made special litter bins for the younger children—the bins lit up when rubbish was put into them. They made funny faces to go over the tops of the ordinary litter bins. They created posters whose message was mainly visual and displayed them in the "infant" areas. On the fifth count they were able to show a reduction in litter in the infant areas also.

Sixth Count—Before their final measurement, the three pupils engaged upon a variety of activities designed to reduce even further the overall litter in the school. They carried out a survey into their classmates' opinions on the causes of litter. They created an imaginary "Litter Chronicle" as a further part of their propaganda. Finally, they invited a spokesman from the local education authority to talk to the school about the general problem of litter in society. The count taken after these activities showed the litter in the school was now reduced to negligible proportions. The girls produced a graph to represent the litter counts on all six occasions, showing the rise to a peak on the second count and the steep decline through the subsequent counts.

It was then near the end of the term so the pupils were unable to measure the long-term effect of their campaign, though they were aware of the possibility that the litter might start to build up again as the effects of the propaganda wore off.

The research team comment that, in effect, the children have been engaged in a small social experiment and their involvement in it seems to have led them to some fruitful insights into social processes.

It is a good example of an opportunity spontaneously developed to encourage children to be involved in the social processes of the school and to participate in responsibility for these processes. In a project such as this much more than simple cognitive ability is involved and we would very much like to see projects similar to this encouraged as opportunities for them arise.[14]

An example of the possibilities of the exchange of ideas by world educators is expressed in the following project on economic education. Although the children involved are ten to eleven years of age, they interacted with and influenced younger children ages five to nine years of age, in their school-wide social experiment. We include this project for its promising practices in the social education of young children and the aspects of the world community of educators it exemplifies.

ECONOMIC EDUCATION PROJECT: REPORT OF A PRIMARY SCHOOL TEACHER

During the last few weeks of the summer term [June and July in 1968], I decided to attempt something entirely different in the field

---

14. Ibid., pp. 72, 105–107, 137–39. This account of the litter project also appears in Denis Lawton, "Maintaining A Supportive Physical Environment of Man: How the Schools May Help," in *Educating the Young People of the World,* edited by A. Miel and L. Berman (Washington D.C.: Association for Supervision and Curriculum Development, 1970), pp. 44–45.

of social studies for junior pupils by introducing my class of ten- and eleven-year-old children to the basic economic facts of life.

In our rapidly expanding technological society, education is seen to play a large part of the kind of "life chance" a child will have, and I felt that children could benefit from seeing, and by being practically involved in experiments which demonstrate the forces at work in their environment. If they can then understand how some of these forces effect them, it may be possible, with re-inforcements at a later stage in their education, for them to manipulate some of these forces to their own advantage. In the lessons on income and why they vary, the children found that generally the better-paying jobs such as engineers, test pilots, and doctors required more training and skill than the lower-paying jobs. Many of them came to realize, through perhaps at this stage internalize, that education can be looked upon as a tool, as it will enable them to produce more later on. Children can then perhaps see that they have educational capital which they can exploit, such as the ability to read, write, and do mathematics. All of these skills could pay handsome dividends and the greater they are developed the larger the pay off.

For the purpose of this work I was guided and indeed gained my first inspiration from the program of economic education that has been devised in America by Professor Lawrence Senesh in collaboration with other academic specialists and with primary school teachers and administrators. After becoming acquainted with the course being used in America, I studied the areas of economic thought that I hoped to cover during the next four weeks, working on some of the more fundamental and practical aspects of economics.

Professor Senesh believes that young children can be taught the basic forms of the society in which they live by relating these forms to their everyday life. One can speculate that young children who get this type of grounding in the junior school will not later be quite so taken in by advertising and appeals to the emotions. Perhaps it may help them to deal rationally and responsibly with some of the problems that affect their well-being and survival, in the complexities of our modern society.

The children were divided into mixed ability groups within whose composition the IQ's ranged from 90 to 140+ and began the project by writing down all the things they would like to own and also those items that they were likely to get. Together we discussed what changes would have to be made in order that their respective wishes could be fulfilled and the children saw that it would involve great industrial expansion; men and a much bigger female labor force, working around the clock, that thousands of acres of arable land would be lost to industry. In this way, the class was introduced to perhaps the most fundamental economic concept concerning the clash between unlimited wants and limited resources. Since man cannot have everything, he must learn to make wise choices.

The groups of children then decided how they would respectively obtain some of the articles listed in their wants column and after discounting unrealistic suggestions, they saw clearly that in order to obtain houses, cars, luxuries and other material things in life, they needed to earn substantial wages or salaries. This discussion led us on to the kind of occupation where high salaries could be obtained and the children studied what kind of qualifications were necessary for well paid jobs such as pilots, engineers, and doctors. They came to see that almost without exception a good education was a necessary investment and that teachers were producers of useful services.

Children can be made aware that the faster and better men can produce goods and services, the more wishes and desires can be fulfilled. They will discover various ways by which goods and services can be produced faster and better. For this purpose I untidied the classroom and asked the class to retidy it. This resulted in everyone trying to do the same job and consequently, without order, the job was done poorly. At their second attempt, where each child was given a specific job to do, the task was carried out speedily and more efficiently. This simple exercise introduced them to the division of labor. In order for them to understand its more sophisticated implications, we attempted to compare two kinds of production techniques.

Two teams produced decorated cakes shaped as rabbits and butterflies. One team worked on the assembly-line principle, where one child mixed the dough, another rolled it out and the next cut it into shape. Finally, the last two members of the team added decorations and packed the finished product into a pan for cooking. In the other team, one child did all the jobs himself. The team using the production line technique almost always produced more cakes and became an efficient team. However, the division of labor was seen to have its disadvantages as the team became bored with their jobs and frustrated at their inability to vary the design.

During subsequent attempts at making cakes, we removed key members from the production line in order to see how the team coped with the inconvenience. After they had experienced early difficulties, the teams reshuffled members so that some could cope with two simple tasks without unduly hindering production. Just at that time a major strike was making news headlines, so I stopped the use of a vital ingredient, flour, where it was assumed that the delivery drivers had gone on strike. Very soon the team realized that production would have to cease and many insightful answers were produced in a piece of written work on the crippling effects of a strike on industry and its side effects elsewhere.

Besides a division of labor, tools play an important part in production, so we timed mixing a given quantity of dough with a wooden spoon, a hand mixer and an electric mixer. The electric mixer was shown to be the most efficient and this demonstrated that efficient, but initially more costly, machinery could release workers for other jobs and save time in the production process.

It took some time for the children to grasp the idea of tools as a form of wealth to be acquired, not for immediate enjoyment, but as a lasting source for additional wealth. From here, we discussed the problems of poor countries who cannot afford quickly to build up capital on the form of expensive tools and machinery.

Our next experiments were designed to show how international trade takes place. We discussed the reasons why most countries cannot or will not produce all the goods and services they would like and therefore have a trade. Then the children set up a primitive system of bartering in which each child offered goods and services to others. The limitations of such a system soon became evident and so money was made in order to improve the system.

Perhaps one of the most useful economic principles became meaningful to the class—the concept of marginal utility—when certain children in a team were each given glasses of lemonade (representing wine from France), sandwiches (representing wheat from Canada), lollipops (representing sugar from Jamaica) and raisins (representing fruit from Africa). The boy who had the glasses of lemonade drank three, leaving others for which he had no use. The girl with ten lollipops thought that four would be enough for her, leaving six uneaten. For the children who owned these goods, only the consumed items had full value, the rest were less useful. It was then left to the children to do as they pleased with the unconsumed items and eventually all goods were exchanged and disposed of. This exercise helped them realize that now all their surplus goods had acquired some kind of value. For the children, by trading now possessed a useful assortment of previously unpossessed goods. I think they were now more acquainted with the concept of world trade having as it were "taken part."

I am hopeful that I may be in a position to try the Science Research Association's Working World Program next academic year with a class of my younger juniors. I would venture to suggest that schools make greater efforts to equip their pupils to understand the complex economic issues of the society in which they live. Economic education can help show the way.[15]

These three projects, "Birth Places," "Litter," and "Economic Education," reviewed by Lawton, Campbell, and Burkitt in their investigations of social studies practices in the British primary schools extensively involved young children in learning about the ways of their society. These same projects could be developed with American children in the early elementary school

---

15. Ibid., pp. 101–104.

years. In fact the Working World series developed by Senesh was prepared for use with children six to nine years of age. It is interesting to note that in the "Litter" and "Birth Places" projects, although the research was initiated and carried out by older primary (elementary) school children, the children involved the youngers—in England the infants school age children of five and six years—as essential contributors to their data and in the results and findings of their investigations.

CHILDREN'S CONCEPTIONS OF AUTHORITY FIGURES

Lawton and Campbell interviewed and tape-recorded more than 100 children during their surveys on the status of social studies in the British primary schools. Two basic social concepts seemed to arise most frequently in the children's discussions with the researchers. These were views on authority and on social stratification. When viewing overall authority figures such as the headmaster (school principal), young children exhibit a high level of sophistication and understanding, Lawton and Campbell feel. They do not see their headmaster or head mistress as a dictator, benevolent or otherwise, ordering teachers and students around. Rather, they construe the role of the headmaster as one of decision-maker. How would American children respond to questions about the role of their elementary school principal? Would we find results or answers like those responses of a nine-year-old British girl that Lawton and Campbell reported?

Q: What sort of decisions would these of the headmaster's be?
A: Well, um, you know, getting new classrooms and things like that; you know; a lot of building. In the spring we had all new toilets, new cloakrooms and all that added on. He has to make decisions about wages, especially with the strike coming along; but um, his job is the hardest of all.
Q: Hardest? Why is that?
A: Well, he has constantly got something to do and it is usually well, deciding, when we should start swimming again at Easter or something like that. Deciding school holidays.
Q: There are lots of decisions he has to make then?
A: Yes, for the whole school, you know. Sometimes he puts his decisions forward at a staff meeting. Mrs._____ [the teacher's name] told us about that. Yes, he puts his decisions forward at a staff meeting, you know, asks around what they think about it.
Q: So he does not make every decision on his own?
A: Yes, he goes round the staff. Or sometimes the teachers come to him with a request.

Lawton and Campbell note that although the children are often inaccurate about facts, such as the headmaster deciding all the issues, they do show insights into the relationships dependent on the authority positions. "Moreover between the adult groups in the school, the children make very fine distinctions about the exercise of authority." Here again a nine-year-old's response to the investigators' questions:

Q: Would a caretaker be able to tell a teacher what to do?
A: No.
Q: Would a teacher be able to tell a caretaker what to do?
A: Well, I suppose so, if she had authority from the headmaster.
Q: Would a teacher be able to tell the school secretary what to do?
A: They would rather ask her if she would do something for them. You know, they would say: "Could you please do this for me tonight if you have got any spare time?"[16]

Lawton, Campbell, and other educators in England believe there is a need to help children understand their own and other societies. They feel that the social education of young children is an essential element of the curriculum. The survey discussed here that investigated unique social studies projects for the middle years of schooling and the new three-year project now underway on the development of teacher-designed curriculum materials to be carried out with selected Teacher Centers in social science for the middle school years reinforces the British Schools Council commitment to social education.

SOCIAL EDUCATION IN THE BRITISH PRIMARY SCHOOLS — THE SCHOOL ASSEMBLY

The general organization and program scheduling in British Primary Schools (this includes infants—five- to seven-year-olds and juniors—seven- to eleven-year-olds) calls for a daily assembly in which all the classes or ("forms," as the British call them) and their teachers are in attendance. The assembly is often given over to the headmaster or mistress as the time to discuss school, neighborhood, and/or community problems, general ethical and moral values, or for time for recognition of outstanding students in scholarship and deportment. Sometimes a particular group of children will present a program they have rehearsed and worked out especially for the assembly. It is an important and meaningful time of the school day for the children and their teachers. Since primary schools are usually 200 to 300 pupils in size, the entire student body can be present together to participate in the ongoing events and discussions.

During my visits to primary schools in London and Birmingham, England, in the spring and summer of 1971, I participated as an honored

16. R. J. Campbell and Denis Lawton, "How Children See Society," *New Society,* November 19, 1970, p. 570–73.

guest and an observer at a number of these assemblies. At the Sir Francis Drake School in the Deptford dock area of London, a very old, lower socioeconomic, working-class sector of London, the headmaster was holding forth at the daily assembly on traffic problems and safety measures for the students of the school. He demonstrated on a chalk board for the group of about 200 children seated on the wooden floor of a large, open room, windowed on three sides to make it airy and sunny. Most of the newer primary schools have these special rooms, much like our large gyms, where "apparatus," climbing and physical education equipment, are used during some part of the school day and stored away at other times. The headmaster discussed with the children, while drawing diagrams on his chalk board, what happens when children run across the street without watching for oncoming cars. He personalized the situation he was describing by naming a parent in the neighborhood as the driver of the car, but kept the student involved in the near mishap as nameless. This headmaster was intimately familiar with all the families, children and adults, of his school and the school's neighborhood. He discussed this point with his American visitors after the assembly, and reiterated how essential this knowledge of the school community was to the adequate fulfillment of his position as headmaster of Sir Francis Drake School.

The Marden Mount School is in the Lewisham district of London on out beyond the Deptford area. There are 325 children in the school whose parents' occupations range from day laborers, and those out of work, to professionals, artists, and teachers. The school is about ten years old and almost adjacent to a large, high-rise housing complex, which the British call "council estates housing." The assembly this day was conducted by one of the teachers, Miss Wilkes. Children were designated to show their art work to the seated classes of children gathered in the large, sunny, central room of the school. The theme for the art work was "Me and My Friends." The children discussed their drawings, saying that "We meet our friends at school where we learn good manners and how to be helpful to each other." Then the children who had birthdays on that day were honored and had a chance to show one of the gifts they received. A paper birthday cake was produced by the teacher-in-charge. The birthday children counted the lighted candles and then blew them out. When the assembly ended the teachers and several infants school "students" (student teachers) led the various classes back to their rooms to continue open style, integrated day organization of the school. Pupils are vertically grouped with five-, six- and seven-year-olds in classes of about 36 children each.

By moving industry outside of London proper, new towns such as Stevenage, have been established. Located about 40 miles from London, Stevenage is typical of the small cities England has created since World

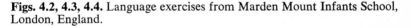

Figs. 4.2, 4.3, 4.4. Language exercises from Marden Mount Infants School, London, England.

War II by dispersing industry and hence the workers. Here one finds a wide range of socioeconomic classes represented in the school population since most residents live in development housing. Lodge Farm Infant School has about 300 children ages five to seven-plus. The school building is new and one is almost immediately impressed with the extensive display of children's art work as one enters the school. Not only is this art work colorful, original, and exciting as one views it on walls, windows, ceilings and halls of the school, but the use of unique materials, many of them gathered from the local factories' surplus or reject materials, creates a dazzling effect.

Figs. 4.5, 4.6, 4.7. Artwork, Lodge Farm Infants School, Stevenage, England.

The assembly time at this school was also different and interesting. Parents had been invited especially for the program that day. The assembly began with the classes of children and their teachers filing into the central room to the music of a Mozart symphony on the record player. The headmistress, Mrs. Roe, began the assembly and gave special welcome to the parents, both mothers and quite a few fathers, as well as a number of younger children who were in attendance. Then the program was turned over to the teacher of a group of five- and six-year-olds. They presented a skit on homes based on the poem, "The House That Jack Built." The children had created beautiful, freehand paintings of homes from various cultures—the American Indian wigwam, the Eskimo igloo, and, of course, the English cottage. When the assembly came to a close the parents and younger children left the assembly room first, then the groups of children with their teachers, some to watch a specially scheduled BBC broadcast on Australia. Teachers and children watch BBC broadcasts together and much of the exciting art work and subject matter in the primary school curriculum is stimulated by this interaction.

Why do we stress that these assemblies of the British primary schools are a form of social education? As pointed out in chapter 1 of this book, the assembly provides a daily situation, a formal ceremony to develop deep ties and feelings of participating in an occasion that brings children and adults together in a reaffirmation of social customs and traditions. Children learn about the ways of their society. Group solidarity is reinforced, since everyone in the school (including teachers, students, student teachers, the headmaster or mistress, and many times the parents and younger siblings) is in attendance and emotionally involved in the ongoing events of the assembly. These events could be as mundane as a discussion of safety rules or the recognition of a child's birthday or a special program put on for the parents, as we have described on the preceding pages.

What has happened to the school assembly in American elementary schools? It has become increasingly more and more a rare occasion. As our schools grow in size to seven hundred, eight hundred, even a thousand children in a traditional K through 6 elementary school, the auditorium, gymnasium, or multi-purpose room cannot possibly hold such a large school population at one sitting. More and more the principal or other individual in charge of special programs will schedule a portion of the classes in the auditorium, usually the first through the third grades, then the fourth, fifth, and sixth grades, will see the entertainment or the movie. The kindergartens are often deleted from the special program with the rationalization that they are too young and would not understand what is going on anyhow. The result is that the wonderful sense of solidarity and belongingness that characterize the British primary school organization is lost in many American elementary schools. And some of this loss can be attributed to the few opportunities for the total student body to assemble together and participate in a group occasion as compared to the British schools, where it occurs every day.

Further, the range of age groups coming together, along with the adults, the teacher and headmaster, all present and contributing to the occasion, is sadly missing from many of the programs held in American schools. Sometimes teachers "sneak" away during an assembly, especially if it is a film where the room is darkened, and do not participate at all. How often is the principal, or even the assistant principal on hand for special occasions in the auditorium or multi-purpose room? When do sixth graders and kindergarteners join together to form an audience or group, so that the youngers can observe the olders and find models for their behavior and role performance? We do not wish to make a blanket indictment of American schools. Rather, we would stress the importance of the all-school gathering, the assembly, in the social education of the young child who is being socialized and enculturated at a crucial time in his emotional and intellectual growth when deep impressions can be aroused and sustained through adulthood.

PROMISING PRACTICES IN THE SOCIAL EDUCATION OF AMERICAN CHILDREN

In order to present a fair assessment of the promising practices in social education of young children, we should look at some of the innovative and outstanding programs in the United States. In 1971 the National Center for Educational Communication made a survey of promising programs in early childhood education. In that survey, several early childhood centers stand out as particularly organized around a social awareness approach. These include the Cross-Cultural Family Center, San Francisco, California, and The Magic Circle—Human Development Model, San Diego, California. Other influential model programs not specifically described in the survey but referred to in the reports are the New Nursery School, Greeley, Colorado; the Toy Lending Libraries, Oakland, California; the Social Science Curriculum of the Kindergarten Guide for Indian Children, Bureau of Indian Affairs.

The Cross-Cultural Family Center. Located in San Francisco, the Family Center is committed to the values of cross-cultural associations for young children. Stated goals for both parents and teachers are:

> a family approach to educating young children;
> development of a positive sense of self-esteem;

development of an appreciation for their own individual uniqueness
and a respect for the individuality of others;
successful cross-cultural experiences through planning and working
together.[17]

The teaching staff of the school is racially mixed and includes males. The
NCEC booklet goes on to state that the activities of the Center are designed
to foster basic trust, autonomy, cognitive development, and social competence. Even four-year-olds notice differences and ask questions. Differences
are discussed and accepted. The Center features celebrations such as Japanese Children's Day, Martin Luther King's birthday, Christmas, and other
special occasions characteristic of diverse cultures and subcultures.

> The school kitchen is an exciting part of the program. Here mothers pre-
> pare soul food, Swedish cookies, fortune cookies, sweet and sour pork,
> Southern fried chicken, special breads and cakes, and many other
> varieties of food. Folk music, art, and stories from many cultures are
> an integral part of the program. Trips to an African shop, a German
> delicatessen, or a Japanese toy store are very special events. For the
> youngsters and their families, cross-cultural associations have become
> an enriching way of life.[18]

Here is a program that stresses social education for very young children, ages two through five years, and incorporates their parents as well.
In assessing the effectiveness of the Cross-Cultural program, both parents
and children were given batteries of tests and questionnaires. The results
indicated that over a three-year period children who participated in the
Family Center Program seemed to be without racial or class prejudice and
parents were more open-minded in accepting members of other socioeconomic and racial groups as friends, in their social life, and in crossing
racial and economic lines.

The Human Development Model. This model is based on a curriculum organized by Harold Bessell and Uvaldo Palomares of the Human
Development Training Institutes of San Diego, California. The following
account of this model in action was recorded by a graduate study in an
early childhood education class. The classroom of four-year-olds is taught
by an experienced kindergarten teacher who was trained in the theory of
the Human Development Model by members of the Institute. The school
where this early childhood program is held is a public school in a large
Southwestern city system, and is located in a lower socioeconomic, mainly
Hispano subculture area.

---

17. National Center for Educational Communication, *Model Programs Childhood
Education: Cross-Cultural Family Center* (Washington, U.S. Dept. of Health, Education and Welfare, Office of Education, 1970), p. 2.
18. Ibid., p. 8.

The account begins:

> One afternoon ten or twelve four-year-old children were asked by their teacher to take hands in a circle and sit down. The teacher, herself, was part of the circle. She rattled a cigar box as the children speculated as to the contents. The box was shown to contain seven pairs of identical objects (squares of wood, straws, scissors, green clothespins, paperclips, macaroni, and arrowheads). Each pair of objects was exhibited with an accompanying "These are two_____. They are exactly the same." The children sat mutely watching, except for one who left the group and returned twice. The teacher then called on each child by name to select two objects which were "exactly the same" from the cigar box. Each child was praised for his performance and none made an error.
>
> The circle broke into segments as excited children attempted to be the next to choose objects from the box. The teacher, however, called only on those who were seated and the circle returned to normal. Next, the teacher chose two objects asking each child by name if the objects were the same or different. None made mistakes and again praise was liberally dispensed. Finally, each child was asked to select an object without looking. The teacher in the meantime held an object behind her back. After the child selected, another child, one seated in the circle, was asked by the teacher, "Are we the same, or are we different?" The objects were held up by the two choosers (teacher and child). Again, each child was praised for his answer and none made an error. The children were told to prepare for various new activities and the circle broke.
>
> The children were participating in the "Magic Circle" created by Harold Bessell for his *Methods in Human Development* model co-authored by Uvaldo Palomares. The "Magic Circle" may be considered a modified encounter group in which young children educate themselves about interpersonal cause and effect relationships, dispel any thought that their experiences are totally unique, and learn to understand emotion. Bessell and Palomares have designed a curriculum which provides for daily "Magic Circle" sessions lasting approximately twenty minutes for children ages four to eight or nine years.[19]

In the theory manual Bessell and Palomares state the purpose of their curriculum: "I wanted to see if effective, large-scale *preventive* measures could be taken that would assure normal, healthy emotional growth, much as a sound, balanced diet can ensure the development of children who are physically normal and healthy. . . . We knew therefore that a soundly based preventive scheme had to focus on three main areas of experience or themes: *awareness* (knowing what your thoughts, feelings, and actions really are), *mastery* (knowing what your abilities are and how to use them), and *social interaction* (knowing other people)."[20]

19. Margaret Kaluk. "A Curriculum for Preventive Mental Health" (unpublished paper for Early Childhood Education, University of Denver, Fall, 1971), pp. 1–2.

20. Harold Bessell and Uvaldo Palomares, *Methods in Human Development Theory Manual* (San Diego, Calif.: Human Development Training Institute, 1970), p. i.

The Human Development model was just recently organized but has already seen success in the San Diego area and is now being adopted by other early childhood programs across the country in cities such as Denver, Colorado, and Seattle, Washington. Specific results of the program are not available at this writing, but the implications for social education are evident from the basic philosophy of the model.

The New Nursery School. The central concept of this early childhood program is the establishment of a self-teaching, self-rewarding, or autotelic environment for learning. The majority of the children at the New Nursery School come from a disadvantaged, impoverished population of Spanish-speaking families living on the outskirts of Greeley, Colorado. The four main goals of the school are: (1) to develop a positive self-image on the part of the child; (2) to develop the child's senses and perceptions; (3) to develop problem-solving and concept-formation ability; and (4) to develop verbal skills. One aspect of this comprehensive program is unique in the use of a form of the "talking typewriter" to promote language development and verbal skills. These typewriters are installed in special booths, small rooms outside the main classroom of school, which is housed in an old frame residence. Observers can watch what the children and the "booth assistant" are doing through the one-way glass that forms a wall of the learning booth.

The booth assistants are usually males or Spanish-speaking college students (female) who work with the children on a one-to-one basis in a tutorial setting within the learning booth. The child is offered the opportunity to work in the booth each day. He can refuse this offer if he chooses, although most of the children enjoy the booth time and even indicate their desire to stay longer. A typical session in the booth might include some typing on the electric typewriter on a particular topic or interest developed by the program's curriculum. The session of about ten minutes also includes discussion and manipulation of toys or other objects in both Spanish and English. In the concept development area of the main room, pictures and objects of current interest for the children are displayed, such things as sugar beets being harvested by their parents in the fall, or sheep's wool that one of the children's father has sheared from a sheep that week. This use of the child's language and the recognition of things that are of economic importance in his family's life are stressed by Oralie McAfee, the head teacher of the New Nursery School.

Mrs. McAfee states that the social education of the young child can be viewed from three separate, yet connected, routes. She sees the first of these as socialization, learning to function as a member of a group, and enculturation or good citizenship in the school setting. From the teacher's standpoint this is classroom management or "discipline." The second route she characterizes as helping the young child to learn about his own community and the culture, or cultures in which he is operating, hence the emphasis on local products and materials as described in the New Nursery classrooms and booths. The third route to social education of the young child deals with appropriate objectives in the social studies disciplines, resources and activities to help children achieve those objectives and a tentative instructional and organizing theory.

Oralie McAfee describes the following scene in her New Nursery classroom:

> Yesterday, I watched a boy from a very disadvantaged home build with blocks a creditable launching pad and two rockets. Using different-sized cylinders, with triangles on top to simulate command modules, he had made a big and "ih-uh 'ocket." Where was he going? Of course. "To the moon." It is so easy to think in terms of what *we* think children should be interested in — the circus, life on the farm, nursery rhymes — that we do not see and hear what those children are actually telling us![21]

This is why we need to carefully plan and organize for the introduction of social education into the curriculum of young children. Adults can so easily underestimate the social awareness of young children because they do not verbalize extensively about the events that are going on around them. Then we give them "going to the grocery store" instead of "rockets to the moon."

The Toy Lending Library. At the Far West Laboratory for Educational Research and Development in Berkeley, California, one of the programs, Education Beginning at Age Three, developed the Parent/Child Toy-Lending Library. The major objectives of the Education Beginning at Age Three program are to incorporate in classroom organization and teaching procedures the following conditions:

1. permit the learner to explore freely;
2. inform the learner immediately about the consequences of his actions;
3. be self-pacing;
4. permit the learner to make full use of his capacity for discovering relations of various kinds;
5. structure is such that the learner is likely to make a series of interconnected discoveries about the physical, culture, or social world.

The program is also responsive to children by taking into account their

21. Oralie McAfee, "Social Studies in the Early Childhood Curriculum," speech made at the National Council for the Social Studies National Conference, Nov. 22, 1971, Denver, Colorado.

cultural backgrounds and life styles. This means using culturally relevant materials whenever possible; encouraging the use of the child's language in school; recognizing that the competencies children have developed may be different depending on their environment and background; these differences should in no way label the children as being "deprived." "Because we recognize the children's ethnic and social backgrounds, we believe that the parents are the ones who are responsible for the education of their children, and that they should be involved in the decisions that affect their children's education.[22]

Nimnicht stresses that although the Education Beginning at Age Three Program works primarily with Head Start, the staff does not want the Toy-Lending Library project to be considered a compensatory program for "deprived" children. The developers see the Toy-Lending Library concept as effective for all three- and four-year-old children. This is because the toys and related episodes were developed as devices to help parents achieve some understanding of the principles of child development and to provide a starting point to promote a desirable interaction between the parent and child.

The Basic Set of toys in the Toy-Lending Library are:

Sound Cans—two sets of small, metal film cans; a set consists of six cans, each one contains a different object such as a bead, water. Each can sounds different when it is shaken. One set is for the parent the other for the child.

Color Lotto—a square wooden board divided into nine differently colored squares and two sets of nine small squares each.

Feely Bag—a drawstring bag and two sets of masonite cutouts consisting of a circle, a square, a triangle, and a rectangle.

Stacking Squares—sixteen wooden squares of four graduated sizes that fit on a wooden spindle. This toy is constructed so that it is self-correcting in the process of stacking.

Wooden Table Blocks—ten sizes

Number Puzzle

Color Blocks—16 small cubic blocks

Flannel Board—36 small felt shapes in different colors.

There is a second series of toys including an alphabet board, a matrix game, coordination board, 100 peg board, inset shapes board, pattern box, property blocks and a spinner boards.

Evaluation of the program has shown that as a result of using the

---

22. Glen P. Nimnicht. "A Report on the Evaluation of the Parent/Child Toy-Lending Library Program" (Berkeley, Calif.: Far West Laboratory for Educational Research and Development, 1971), p. 10.

Toy-Lending Library parents feel more competent in helping their children learn what they believe to be important skills and concepts; feel that they can influence the decisions that affect the education of their children; have a better understanding of what their child is capable of learning and, therefore, a feeling that he can be successful. As a result of this, the child increases his competency because of the interaction with the parents.[23]

Here is an exciting approach that involves parents directly in the education and early training of concepts and skills in their child. The Toy-Lending Library functions within the arrangement of an educational course for the parents taught, or rather directed, by a teacher-librarian trained by the Far West Laboratory. The Toy-Lending Library program goes far beyond the usual suggestions of educators that teachers of young children try to mention to parents that the type of toys they purchase for their children is very important. An example of this is reflected in the writing of a British educational sociologist who says that "At one extreme a mother may regard toys simply as 'something that children have.' Alternatively, she may see them as an indispensable aid to the child's development."[24]

Rather than merely talking at parents, the Toy-Lending Library is an action program that provides carefully developed toys and well-organized training built upon child development principles with which parent and child can interact. The ramifications for child socialization in such a practice are impressive.

Kindergarten Curriculum Guide for Indian Children. Though the Curriculum Guide could not be labeled an on-going program for young children, it does present some promising practices in integrating social education into the kindergarten curriculum of a unique group of children— those attending the Bureau of Indian Affairs day schools on or near Indian reservations. The *Kindergarten Curriculum Guide* was developed by educators at the Bank Street College of Education, the National Association for the Education of Young Children, and the Bureau of Indian Affairs. In specifically discussing the development of social science concepts, the Guide states:

> Neglect of the cultures of the American Indian is destroying his heritages, and his tribal patterns. In non-Indian schools, children frequently study "the Indians." For the child growing up in the context of the reservation, it becomes the task of the school to help him develop options for his future life. He must be helped to develop a healthy self concept that respects, admires and carries forth his culture.[25]

23. Ibid., p. 4.
24. Jean Jones, "Social Class and the Under-Fives," *New Society*. December 22, 1966, p. 150.
25. U.S. Bureau of Indian Affairs, *A Kindergarten Guide for Indian Children: A Bilingual-Bicultural Approach*, Curriculum Bulletin no. 5 Division of Curriculum and Program Review (Washington, D.C., 1970), p. 82.

Suggestions for teaching social studies include the following ideas and topics:

In planning trips to visit ruins and gathering artifacts for the classroom (to further enhance the child's understanding of his heritage and tribal tradition), teachers should be alert to cultural taboos.

Studying the World of Work.—Today the American Indian is employed at a large variety of jobs. A few of the many occupations available and an example of the tribe known for it are:

Farmers: Cherokees, Sioux
Herders: Navajo, Hopi
Forestry: Cherokee, Seminole, Utes
Sawmill: Navajo, Chippewa
Reindeer herding: Togisk Eskimos
Ranching: Apache, Blackfeet
Fisherman: Haidas
Construction: Mohawk
Fire Fighters: Zuni, Hopi, Mescalero Apache
Oil Drilling: Osage, Oklahoma
Road Construction: Eskimos
Carpenters: Cherokee, Sioux, Hopi

The importance of the role of craftsmen is also stressed, such as the Navajo silversmith, the Pueblo drum-maker, the Hopi potter. Rug-weaving, basket-making, and the creation of sandpaintings are described and suggestions for use in the kindergarten curriculum of these specialized Indian crafts are urged. "The microcosm of a tribal society with its own idiosyncratic patters must be given consideration, even though these roles are duplicated in the larger society. In some instances, both the medicine man and the pediatrician are consulted when a child is ill."[26] Other topics the Guide lists for the social studies area are housing, transportation, and foods and cooking, and each is carefully related to Indian reservation life.

It is pointed out that most American children hear a simple phrase like "Good morning" every day at home and on the streets, but Navajo children do not. Furthermore, the very words "good morning" are completely alien and unthinkable to the Navajo child. To say these words and look right in a person's eyes is considered impolite, according to the Navajo way of life. The Guide suggests therefore, that as one of the Navajo child's first musical experiences the teacher try the changing of a typical Navajo vocable (no-meaning sounds) and then add a child's name, rather than the traditional kindergarten good morning song. For example: A YEH YANGA, A YEH YANGA . . . A YEH YANGA, A YEH YANGA,

---

26. Ibid., pp. 83–85.

LORENZO, ANGA. Note: First, pick a comfortable pitch for the base tone. Then say A, as in fate, prolonging the sound. Then, intone or chant the syllables to a rhythmic beat, walking speed, saying each syllable rather short and curt. YANGA, sound like kong-ah, only substitute the "Y" consonant sound. There will be a little dip on the second YANGA. Listen for this; try to imitate.[27]

The Bureau of Indian Affairs *Kindergarten Curriculum Guide* represents a new approach, the bilingual-bicultural perspective as significant in early learning. By recognizing the child's cultural heritage when he first enters the school setting, the Guide builds upon what the child brings to school rather than ignoring or negating that which has been of central importance in the life of a five-year-old up to now. Traditionally, the stance of the B.I.A. boarding and day schools has been to extoll the "white man's ways" to the Indian child on the rationalization that the Indian must be assimilated into modern American life and give up his tribal ways eventually. Now in 1970 the *Kindergarten Curriculum Guide* specifically states as the philosophy of the Kindergarten: "The Kindergarten is the bridge between home and school—a place where the young child and his family feel comfortable and at home, where value is put on *him*: his culture, his enthusiasm, his drives and interests. . . . The kindergarten program builds on strengths the child brings with him and extends the base upon which the following years of schooling will rest."[28] As American society moves toward truly becoming a pluralistic, multicultural nation, the educational enterprise is called upon to recognize and then utilize ethnic diversities. Education can no longer function as a "melting pot" assimilating all comers into a mass society. The voices of minority groups, Indians among them, are being heard across the land shouting for equal representation and recognition before the law in economic opportunities, in political and social life, and in the educational enterprise, as well. The B.I.A. *Kindergarten Curriculum Guide* is a harbinger of this awakening of the American conscience as reflected in so simple (but tremendously significant) a suggestion as greeting the Indian kindergartener with "A YEH YANGA, LORENZO" rather than "Good morning, Lorenzo." The practice of recognizing and using diversity of customs and folkways applies not only to multicultural populations within our country, but to the broader world culture as well.

---

27. Ibid., p. 128.
28. Ibid., pp. 1–2.

PUTTING WORLDMINDEDNESS IN THE EARLY CHILDHOOD CURRICULUM

We need to begin early in the education of the child to prepare him to live in a multicultural society and a world culture. Worldmindedness means a sense of global responsibility. This can only stem from a positive sense of self and a regard for one's own traditions, customs, and the ways of one's people. If children can be socialized with the feelings that they are the bearers of a proud heritage, then they can extend this sense of belonging to others in the creation of a brotherhood of all mankind. This would be a road to the elimination of otherness, the philosophy men have held for so many centuries that *"we* are the people" and "they" are less than human so we have the right to destroy them. The concept of a world community of educators heralds the development of worldmindedness in the curriculum. We are calling for beginning the teaching of world perspectives in early childhood education and not holding back until the later years of elementary school or waiting for the child to reach the secondary-school levels.

It *is* possible to teach about worldmindedness in the early childhood curriculum. We have cited projects and programs both in England and in

Fig. 4.8. "My Principal"—Debbie, age six, Stevens School, Denver, Colorado. (Courtesy Trudy Katzman.)

the United States that involve young children in social education, social awareness, and multicultural perspectives in the daily activities of their learning experiences. Teachers of young children will vigorously assert that they do have cross-cultural and multi-ethnic programs when at Christmas time they celebrate the holiday in many lands, or build a globe and put "Santa at the North Pole." But we would point out that this type of program in the nursery school and kindergarten is really quite superficial. The early childhood education programs we described in the United States all stem from a basic philosophy and from a curriculum grounded in and built around cross-cultural, multi-ethnic social education. The British projects, also, integrate social education and a worldwide view of society into every aspect of the daily school program—into the reading, mathematics, social studies, science, art, and music of the child's curriculum. Further, olders are intimately involved in teaching youngers, and thereby developing a sense of social solidarity.

In early childhood education in the decade just past, we have been so concerned with compensatory programs for teaching language development, verbal skills, and cognitive learning that we have all but ignored the crucial area of the affective domain, the social education of the young child.

Sources

Bessell, Harold and Palomares, Ulvaldo. *Methods in Human Development Theory Manual.* San Diego, Calif.: Human Development Training Institute, 1970.

King, Edith. *The World: Context for Teaching in the Elementary School.* Dubuque, Ia.: Wm. C. Brown Co., Publishers, 1971.

Lawton, Denis. "Social Sciences in the Schools." *New Society.* London, England (April 25, 1968).

Lawton, Denis; Campbell, R. J.; and Burkitt, Valerie. Report to the Schools Council — subsequently published as Schools Council Working Paper Number 39, *Social Studies 8-13.* London: Evans, Methuen Educational, 1971. Distributed in the United States by Citation Press, p. 7, 76-79.

McAfee, Oralie. "Selected Evaluation of an Approach to Early Childhood Education," in Preschool Programs for the Disadvantaged. ed. J. Stanley. Baltimore: Johns Hopkins University Press, 1972.

Miel, Alice, and Keister, E. *The Shortchanged Children of Suburbia.* New York: Institute of Human Relations Press, 1967.

——————, and Berman, Louise. *Educating the Young People of the World.* Washington: Association for Supervision and Curriculum Development, 1970.

National Center for Educational Communication. *Model Programs of Childhood Education.* Washington, D.C.: U.S. Department of Health, Education, and Welfare, Office of Education, 1970.

Nimnicht, Glenn. "A Report on the Evaluation of the Parent/Child Toy-Lending Library Program." Berkeley, Calif.: Far West Laboratory for Educational Research and Development, 1971.

Rogers, Vincent. *Teaching in the British Primary School*. New York: The Macmillan Co., 1970.

Taylor, Harold. *The World as Teacher*. Garden City, N.Y.: Doubleday & Co., Inc., 1969.

U.S. Bureau of Indian Affairs. *A Kindergarten Guide for Indian Children*. Curriculum Bulletin no. 5. Washington, D.C.: U.S. Government Printing Office, 1970.

Weber, Lilian. *The English Infant School and Informal Education*. Englewood Cliffs, N.J.: Prentice Hall, 1972.

Zolotow, Charlotte. *You and Me*. New York: The Macmillan Co., 1971.

chapter 5

Toward a Sociology of Early Childhood Education

Throughout this book we have attempted to show how teachers of young children can find the sociological perspective useful in their teaching, in developing the curriculum of early childhood education, and in analyzing what is occurring daily in the classroom, in the school, and in the broader community. This is a relatively new and little explored area for sociology and for early childhood education as well. Recently a few sociologists have turned to looking at the educational enterprise in new and exciting ways. One of these sociologists is Sarane Boocock of the University of Southern California, best known in educational circles for her pioneering work in educational games and simulations. In *An Introduction to the Sociology of Learning* Boocock points out that surprisingly little sociological attention has been directed toward the major function of schools—the learning environment. Rather, sociologists tend to study the bureaucratic nature of school organizations in structural-functionalist orientation. A number of studies have been directed toward the social origins or teachers and/or administrators, but only since the impact of desegregation and the need for integration of public schools under court order has much attention been paid to ethnic and racial affiliation, as well as social class, upon the learning environment in the classroom and in the school. Boocock states that the premise of her book on the sociology of learning, is that *sociology* has a contribution to make which is independent of psychological learning theory so dominant in the field since the 1920s. She writes: "This book explores a relatively new field or subfield of sociology. Its subject is the learning enviroment, which includes the social characteristics of schools and their surroundings, and the student's relationships with other individuals and groups, inside and outside of school, that effect his academic sucess."[1]

---

1. Sarane Spence Boocock, *An Introduction to the Sociology of Learning* (Boston: Houghton Mifflin Co., 1972), pp. 3–4.

Fig. 5.1. Self-portrait, five-year-old, University Park Elementary School Kindergarten, Denver, Colorado.

With this final chapter we intend to join Boocock in adding to the growing body of writing that applies sociological theory to educational theory and practice. However, our emphasis is on the uses of sociological theory for those working with young children, ages three to eight years, also a field that has been dominated by psychology and more or less avoided in sociology.

THE USES OF SOCIOLOGY FOR EARLY CHILDHOOD EDUCATION

We began in the first chapter to describe the social climate of the classroom of young children. We investigated the quality of interpersonal relations in groups of young children where teachers are the leaders and authority figures. We saw how the classroom as a social arena can function in an atmosphere of distrust and even viciousness or in an atmosphere of security and trust. Now new materials and writings on interpersonal relations in the classroom and in the school are becoming available to teachers to help them in improving human interaction in the educational setting. One such book is Elizabeth Hunter's *Encounter in the Classroom: New Ways of Teaching.* This book presents ways in which teachers can change their patterns of questioning, calling for imagination and thought on the part of students rather than merely recall and retrieval of information. Hunter suggests ways that teachers can expand the amount of pupil talk, and pupil-to-pupil interaction that considers feelings and emotions as well as cognitive information. *Encounter in the Classroom* describes techniques for encouraging students to share in decision-making power in areas that bear on their daily school life. This power in the decision-making process extends from student to teacher to administrator so that more than just lip-service is paid to the democratic process in American schools. This book stresses processes in which students and teachers can find success working with others rather than gaining achievement at the expense of others. Hunter writes about "the establishment of a climate that encourages pupils to say 'I need help' without worrying about jeopardizing thier careers; the establishment of a spirit among school personnel that inspires them to work together to improve learning conditions for children."[2]

Hunter's book is one of the new genre of writings that provides specific and detailed techniques for an open, democratic social climate in classrooms of children, and especially for young children and their teachers.

Particularly in classrooms for young children do teachers have a tendency to do all the planning, organizing, and then evaluating of the program in what could be construed as a most authoritarian manner. But if the teacher thinks in terms of the democratic philosophy espoused by John Dewey, kindergarteners and even pre-schoolers can be involved in the planning, decision-making, and evaluation in early childrood classrooms. Discussion sessions where the teacher places ideas before the children, really listens to their suggestions and reactions, clarifies and incorporates their ideas, and culminates the planning or evaluation session by developing a chart story or plan brings this democratic model to life. Then posting the written plan for all to see—even if they cannot actually read the material—and allowing and encouraging student-initiated action based on the chart plan, brings into actualization the democratic social climate in the classroom.

The uses of sociology in early childhood education were applied to an examination of power and status relations in the classroom. This is often termed "discipline" or "classroom management" by traditional educators

---

2. Elizabeth Hunter, *Encounter in the Classroom: New Ways of Teaching* (New York: Holt, Rinehart & Winston, Inc., 1972), pp. 16–17.

or, in more social scientific terminology, the "ethnography of the class-room," the "culture of the school." However, when construed in a sociological perspective, we see that some individuals are subordinated (usually students) while other individuals in the school are dominant (usually the teachers and administrators). Yet life in classrooms does not have to be demeaning or belittling for those in positions of subordination. If the school and the classroom groups function with mutual respect for all members of the group, then opinions and ideas can be expressed and valued even from the five-year-old. For example, the following anecdote about a teacher and her class of multi-aged children shows regard for original thinking even from the youngest member of the group.

This group of children had just returned from a field trip to the top of a nearby mountain. The children with their teacher were discussing the phenomenon of finding only low-growing, scrubby trees at the top of the mountain. Several theories and explanations were offered. A five-year-old boy who was with the group offered this explanation: There really were very tall trees at the top of the mountain but they had such a long way to grow up through the mountain that just their tops were showing. He cited as evidence for this theory pieces of root at the base of the mountain, which he pointed out to the teacher. Neither the teacher nor the older children in the group laughed or belittled the five-year-old's theory. Rather they praised him for his creative thinking and keen observation of the natural elements on the field trip just completed.[3]

Sociology helps us to visualize the routines of the early childhood classroom as rituals of socialization. The rules and regulations of the school socialize and enculturate the child into membership in his society and, according to Durkheimian sociology, this is moral education. With such a sociological perspective in mind, teachers of the young children recognize an opportunity to shape the citizens of the future who will live in a world that is either egalitarian and democratic or totalitarian and autocratic.

In the second chapter of this book we presented theories developed from dramaturgic sociology and applied them to the learning environment in early childhood classrooms. We focused on the writings of Erving Goffman, on how one presents himself to others in daily interactions, how one really puts on a performance to influence those others, all the while that this performance reflects back, informing the self of adequacies or inadequacies. Sociology is the study of men in groups. One never performs alone. So our exploration of dramaturgic sociology in application to early childhood education led us to examining "performance teams"

3. Edward A. Chittenden, "Notes on Visits to Primary Schools in England," *Outlook*, no. 4 (Winter, 1971), p. 20.

where the "others" form an audience. The team can be adults with the audience of children, or adults and children, or the children can make up the performance team playing out their "drama" in the setting with its front and back regions. Goffman's dramaturgic model is highly flexible and fits situations regardless of the age of performers or their status and power positions.

We went on to see how the performance can become blemished and the individual carry a stigma in the eyes of the group. Goffman's theory of stigmas as the management of spoiled identities was applied to various types of young children just beginning their school careers. The educational enterprise attempts to placate and to adjust children labeled as "special educational problems" by rationalizing their stigmatized situation in what Goffman calls "cooling the mark out," in the terminology of confidence men. Even in early childhood we single out some members of our society for victimization, stigmatizing their lives and their future options by the label, "Special Education." Here the power of the sociological perspective can give us new insights and understandings on the impact and meaning of labels and categories placed on the individual early in life.

This led us to examining the deep sensitivity and awareness of the young child to his social climate, his group affiliation, and his broader culture. In chapter 3 we looked at how the young child is socialized and early in life is aware of social status, sex stereotypes, and sex role identity. The child in turn is not only acted upon, he acts upon others. The young child learns how to cope with socializing agents, developing mechanisms of behavior for handling the many inputs thrust at him daily by his socializers. The importance of play and games of early childhood was discussed from a sociological viewpoint. Here the child has the opportunity to try on the adult roles in the society, to feel what it is like to have power and status, to make decisions and influence others' behavior.

Early childhood teachers have always been aware of the central role of learning to read. Reading is a major force in the educational process. But now, as never before, we are beginning to realize how learning to read permeates all areas of the curriculum—the traditional, academic curriculum and the affective, emotional "hidden" curriculum, also. The impact of reading materials, especially those first primers and workbooks, filled with the stereotypes that mirror the social values of middle-class America, deeply affect the child's motivation in learning to read, and thereby, learning the ways of his society, his group of people.

Until just recently minority children and children from lower socio-economic classes were hard put to find themselves, their life styles, or their family's ways and customs reflected in the primers, first readers, and storybooks they found in their schools. Not only are minority children discriminated against by readers and storybooks, but sex-role stereotypes are rigid and unbending, placing girls and women in insignificant, passive, or nonentity positions in the stories read or told to young boys and girls. An important factor in sociological theory is the effect of socioeconomic status (SES) upon the individual. In chapter 3 we pointed out that little writing or investigation has been done on the impact of socioeconomic status upon early socialization in sex-role behavior and eventual career choices and opportunities. With our dynamic society currently in turmoil over women's rights and women's roles, there seem to be many implications for the sex-role socialization of young children, boys and girls from all sectors of the society, lower-, middle-, and upper-middle-classes. New options and new careers are now on the horizon as men begin to achieve as teachers of young children, and women begin to find success in assertive, leadership positions in education.

Nor only are we experiencing sweeping changes in American culture, we are also rapidly moving toward a world culture. The education of young children now must include a world view, what is termed "world-mindedness," a sense of global responsibility. American children can no longer be socialized with stereotypic images of "foreign" people with strange ways and peculiar customs. To move from a view of America as a multicultural, pluralistic nation to conceptualizing world society in the same terms seems an easy step—and so it will be if we can present American culture to young children as a culture that regards, recognizes, and values differences, allowing its citizens a range of options and practices.

Educators from all over the world are coming together today to discuss educational problems and concerns and to share their research, their theories, and their practices. It is through this world community of educators, particularly the early childhood educators who voice the deep concern and attention that nations around the globe are directing toward the education of the young, that we can hope for significant advances in our field. Sociology has a place in the young child's curriculum providing the tools for shaping the child's social awareness. Now that we have ample evidence he is cognizant of the social phenomena going on around him, we can help him understand what he is experiencing. Sociology can provide the methods and techniques with which children can analyze the customs, traditions and rules of their group, their local community, the larger region, their nation, and even world politics. Children are capable of this intellectual effort, as the British social studies projects demonstrated.

The sociological perspective can provide teachers and administrators with important information and techniques about building group solidarity and rapport. In chapter 4, illustrations and examples were cited from both British and American sources of how sociological principles were instrumental in the education of young children and the formulation of early childhood curriculum. The uses of sociology are many and varied in their application to early childhood education, for student use, for teacher use, for the administrator, for the educator designing the curriculum, for the development of curriculum materials and for the production of audiovisual aids and multimedia materials.

The View Through the Window. In the final chapter of his book, *Humanity and Modern Sociological Thought,* R. P. Cuzzort details the uses of sociological thought. He characterizes sociology as an exciting career, or as broadening one's perspectives and understandings in any career one might follow. But if one does not plan to become a social scientist or follow a scholarly career, sociological knowledge can be applied to many commonplace events. "To the extent that we can understand the influence of social forces, we are more likely to use than be used by society."[4]

An anecdote Professor Cuzzort tells adroitly illustrates the application of sociology to commonplace events. In a lecture to an educational sociology course, he described his recent tour of the new, contemporarily-designed Denver Art Museum, recounting how he and his companion were viewing the various exhibits in the building when they turned a corner on the third level of the building. His companion stopped suddenly and exclaimed "Just look at that!" Cuzzort stopped also and looked but could only see an oddly-placed window. He was puzzled by what his companion seemed to be viewing with expressions of "Oh's" and "Ah's!"

"Look at how perfectly the foothills and the Front Range are framed in that window. The architect did a remarkable job of placing that window in just the right position to catch the visitor's eye with such a striking view, just as he turns this corner," his companion exclaimed.

Cuzzort responded, "Is that what you see? I see just a parking lot filled with cars and a busy downtown city street!" Professor Cuzzort is six feet, four inches tall; his companion was five feet, six inches.

The window of the museum had been positioned appropriately for people of average adult height to just frame the magnificent view of the Colorado Rockies. Those who were much taller, or those who were much shorter, such as young children, were not able to see what the architect had intended.

How did our sociologist, Cuzzort, apply this incident at the museum to sociological thought? His analogy was this: as we function in society, in our daily interactions with people, we view the social scene from our

---

4. R.P. Cuzzort, *Humanity and Modern Sociological Thought* (New York: Holt, Rinehart & Winston, Inc., 1969), p. 324.

vantage point. But sometimes we miss the view through their "windows" if we cannot scrunch down lower or reach up higher to make ourselves figuratively either shorter or taller in order to see their view through the window. Every day those who work with young children are urged to be aware of this need to be flexible, to try to see through the child's eyes the powerful, authoritative, giant-sized adult world. Sociology can aid us in this flexibility.

SOCIOLOGICAL VIEWS OF POWER: IMPLICATIONS FOR EARLY CHILDHOOD EDUCATION

Not only does sociology offer the individual a flexibility of viewpoints and a multiplicity of perspectives in his analysis of social interaction, but within the discipline itself there is an elasticity in the application of concepts and theories to the problems of society. So far in this book we have used the sociological concepts of status and power mainly in the context of small group interaction, in the context of wielding power in the classroom, or the peer group, or within the intimate family setting. This is the emphasis in dramaturgic sociology, the representing of the self to others in daily life, in the fact-to-face interaction with others. Yet, sociology is the study of people's behavior in groups, large and small. While dramaturgic sociology is a relatively new direction for sociological theory, the more classical approach emphasized the structural-functionalism that analyzes the power relationships in the broader society. Sociologists describe society as comprised of institutions—the family, the church, the military, the government, the business men and so on.

One well-known sociologist who wrote extensively on the role of big business, the government and the military was C. Wright Mills.[5] He theorized that among the institutions of society, the major power and decision-making was exerted by the government, the military, and the big business organizations, while the institutions of the school, the church and the family were passive, weak in power, and continually dominated by the power elite—business, government, and the military. Mills felt that governmental agencies were not effective in regulating the activities of business, while another sociologist, Talcott Parsons, contends that the government has displayed effective control over business. This has led to greater power and decision-making ability resting in governmental agencies.[6]

Just as we have advocated the sociological perspective as useful to

---

5. C. Wright Mills, *The Power Elite* (New York: Oxford Press, 1956).

6. Talcott Parsons, *Structure and Process in Modern Societies* (Glencoe, Ill.: The Free Press, 1960).

teachers of young children in understanding and dealing with the culture of the school, so do we feel that the uses of sociology can help teachers contend with the complex political, social, and economic scene where our national priorities are examined and thrashed out. To reiterate Cuzzort's words, the greater understanding we have of social forces, the more options we have to exert pressures to bring our opinions to bear on decisions and regulations.

Look at the case of the Head Start Program over the past decade. Suddenly everyone jumped on the early childhood education bandwagon and advocated early intervention programs as the panacea for all the nation's ills. Head Start's brief history of ups and downs could be viewed as a case of the influence of power and decision-making by specialized interest groups. In 1965 it was hailed as the answer to overcoming disadvantagement of poverty and minority groups, not only in education but in almost all other areas of social welfare and family assistance. By 1967 studies began to appear that contested this grandiose assertion, and called for more realistic perspectives on early education and intervention programs. By 1969 Head Start found itself transferred out of the Office of Economic Opportunity into an expanded Office of Child Development that had once been occupied only by the Children's Bureau. Now have we come full circle, as some politicians' recent statements seem to indicate, to say let us just forget about early education and move now to emphasizing the adolescent and early years of adulthood in the human growth and development cycle?

Advocates and educators dedicated to the field of early childhood will cry out loudly and clearly "Never!" Only by functioning on the most knowledgeable and sophisticated level of social scientific expertise can early childhood advocates hope to hold their own in the cross currents and swirling waters of public political opinion and policy-making. This is why knowledge of the sociological method seems so imperative for us.

The early childhod education issue is not unlike the environmental issue, with claims and counter-claims, and bills being proposed in the Congress advocating this or prohibiting that. Much sound and fury, much publicity, but in actuality a meager amount of legislation requiring action on this deeply disturbing problem in our society. One social scientist commenting on the confused state of the analysis of the enviromental issue offers an explanation that can also be applied to early childhood education. Professor Irving Morrissett, Executive Director of the Social Science Education Consortium at the University of Colorado, writes, "A certain amount of the literature on the environmental problem might well be called "eco-evangelism"—the ardent propounding of solutions accompanied by little or no analysis of causes of, alternatives to, or results of the solutions."[7] If one transposes this concept onto early childhood education, one comes up with a term like "e.c.e.-evangelism"—the ardent support of early childhood programs and intervention strategies with little or no analysis of the causes, alternatives or results. The emotional approach that if it is for little children, it must be good. So we can see how early childhood educators must thread a course between the Scylla of the total rejection of early education and the Charybdis of "e.c.e.-evangelism," in order to present rational and meaningful programs to legislators and to the public.

PRIORITIES OF THE OFFICE OF CHILD DEVELOPMENT — A NEW APPROACH IN THE '70s

How have the shifts in the power structure effected governmental agencies such as the Office of Child Development? A sociological approach will help us understand the controversy around the effectiveness of early childhood research and demonstration projects that has led the Office of Child Development to change its philosophy in the funding of programs and research studies. As the economy of American society enters a recessionary period, governmental spending comes under more careful surveillance by other institutions in the society, particularly by politicians representing big business interests. It is no longer sufficient for the research community to hand in its ideas to the funding agencies, the process used during the 1960s. Now with American society reacting to the changes in the economy and the Congress reflecting these attitudes, the Office of Child Development and other governmental agencies are calling for directed research, projects that are developed in accordance with specific priorities listed by the funding agencies. The staffs of the agencies are asked to come up with a list of priority areas. Parties interested in preparing proposals for these priorities are apprised of the guidelines and deadline dates for submission. Unsolicited proposals in areas not related to priorities rarely have a chance of support, as agency officials tend to make clear in discussions and regional meetings.

For example, the priorities for fiscal year 1972 from the Office of Child Development's Research and Demonstration Unit were:

> *Day Care* (a number one priority)—Development of model day care with emphasis upon child development. These models need not be for poor children only, but can also provide programs for middle-class children.
> *Advocacy* (a number one priority)—Demonstrations of alternative mechanisms for child advocacy at the local level.

---

7. Irving Morrissett, "A Framework for Environmental Education," mimeographed (Social Science Education Consortium, Boulder, 1972), p. 2.

Racism—Study and develop early childhood intervention programs that deal directly with racism. Develop and utilize the talents, skills, and experience of ethnic investigators; develop programs with black colleges and ethnic-operated research groups to familiarize and assist them in engaging in Office of Child Development Research and Evaluation programs. This could include such problems as: How does one train a staff to deal with individual differences in sex, cultural differences, age? How does one teach respect for difference? How does one develop curriculum materials and teaching methods in this area?

Parent Education—Study of child development and child care for teenagers combined with meaningful cross-age relationships; special comprehensive programs for pregnant, school-age girls; demonstration parent education programs for mothers in a variety of settings, including the home and public pediatric clinics.

Father Absence—Demonstrations to provide a male identity for fatherless homes; comparison of effectiveness of volunteers, older adolescents, young adults, college students, and retirees in providing children with male identity and role.

Socioeconomic Mix—Demonstration of preschool programs that include children from all social and economic groups rather than just poverty groups. This includes age, sex, cultural differences. What is the optimum mix? How much of a mix can a teacher handle? How many handicapped children can be handled in such a group?

Television—Research on the impact of television on the infant, preschool child and family, and comparison of the effectiveness of various technological developments, curriculum variations, and scheduling.

Children's Institutions—Demonstrations of methods to bring about change in the institutional care of children.

Adoption—Demonstration to increase the availability of homes for children who are hard to place due to conditions of physical or mental handicap, age, ethnic identity, or institutional residence.

Emergency Services—Demonstration of viable alternatives for the child faced with a traumatic home situation, process of removal from the home, and agency coordination to assist in this process.[8]

All of these priorities seem worthy and urgent concerns of those working with young children. Some of these priorities strongly reflect the ideas and theories in the sociological perspectives on early childhood education presented in this book. But the sociologist would question the closedness and rigidity of the new framework of funding agencies to consider only those proposals that fit the priorities established by the governmental agencies. Society must then depend on the knowledge, breadth, and experience of the staffs of the agencies to prepare lists of priorities that are accurate reflections of the national needs. A heavy task for any group of people, and one that seems to carry too much responsibility when it concerns the future of generations of Americans.

---

8. Department of Health, Education and Welfare, Office of Child Development, mimeographed, 1972.

STATEWIDE SUPPORT OF EARLY CHILDHOOD EDUCATION

We have been examining a view of early childhood education and the early childhood issue from the federal government perspective. Now let us see how those at another level in the power structure, at the state level, consider priorities and issues in the early childhood field. After an analysis of federal priorities and program, the Task Force on Early Childhood Education of the Education Commission of the States reports that it will be up to the states to carry the major burden of early childhood programs and to coordinate their efforts with the many ongoing federally supported programs. The Task Force found that over 300 federal programs for young children were being administered by 18 different federal agencies. This seemed to point to the need for coordinated state planning to take over much of the federal load in the near future.

The Task Force on Early Childhood of the Education Commission of the States has outlined some functions for the administration of early childhood programs at the state level. They suggest the following:

> a. to supervise all state and federal funds for early childhood programs;
> b. to analyze, make recommendations about and coordinate all state and federally funded programs for the development of early childhood personnel;
> c. to develop a master plan for early childhood programs, staff and funding across the state;
> d. to analyze and develop recommendations for state certification efforts related to early childhood personnel;
> e. to develop a system of early diagnosis of children's needs and of parental training and involvement in their children's education;
> f. to make recommendations regarding state standards for private, particularly franchised, early childhood programs;
> g. to serve as an advocate and promoter of programs to meet the needs of all young children in the state and to stimulate the development of post-secondary and inservice training programs for early childhood personnel.[9]

The Education Commission of the States expressed concern over the training and certification of early childhood personnel. They write that for the effective implementation of the state-wide programs a new type of professional early childhood educator will be required. To meet personnel needs for early childhood education programs, they urge the states to establish credentials in early childhood education or at least provide for a strong specialization in early childhood education within the preparation of an elementary certificate, as well as the establishment of the same salary

---

9. Education Commission of the States, Task Force on Early Childhood Education, *Early Childhood Development: Alternatives for Program Implementation in the States* (Denver: 1971), pp. 5–6.

schedules, fringe benefits and tenure rights for early childhood teachers as for all other teachers.[10]

Further, the Task Force's report calls attention to the fact that there is a growing surplus of teachers and Ph.D.'s but hastens to add that this should not be considered an easy solution for filling preprimary positions.

> The key point is that teachers and administrators for early childhood education require qualifications and training different from their counterparts working with older children. Certification procedures and teacher training programs should reflect this fact. For example, for the effective implementation of the program alternatives outlined in this report, a new type of professional early childhood educator will be required. Because emphasis should be on the full development of very young children in a variety of environments but particularly in the home and with the family, the early childhood specialist must be able to muster and coordinate all the resources needed to foster full human effectiveness, wherever they may be located. At their best, such specialists will be sufficiently free from direct administrative ties to be able to help parents and children get better services from all existing agencies, to arrange for services not yet provided and to assist policy-makers in strengthening legislation and administrative structures. In many cases, they will be expected to perform difficult diagnostic functions to determine which youngsters may need more intensive attention before first grade.[11]

Here we have an element of the power structure, governmental officials at the state level, recognizing an urgent need caused by social change. Sociological theory points out that there is often a lag—a cultural lag—when social change occurs. As in the case of programs for action in early childhood education, the society has undergone striking changes in the past two decades, but we are still functioning under a cultural lag, ignoring the pressing needs for universal education of children under six years of age.

These are bold proclamations coming from a source that represents state officials and state funding sources, rather than the federal government. *Early Childhood Development: Alternatives for Program Implementation in the States* contains ideas on possible action states could take in establishing state-wide programs for three-, four- and five-year-olds. The booklet contains information on how to fund such programs and suggestions for implementation. There are three appendices: one outlines educational programs and goals for young children; the second summarizes the proposed federal legislation which President Nixon vetoed in December of 1971; and the third appendix contains tables and graphs showing state funding and personnel programs in early childhood development. From these tables the fact stands out that only six states and American Samoa

---

10. Ibid., p. 9.
11. Ibid., pp. 55–56.

provide some form of support for pre-kindergarten programs, and only eleven states require state certification for day-care personnel. The lack of higher education institutions offering advanced degrees in early childhood education is also evident from a perusal of the tables. One hopes that there will be wider distribution of *Early Childhood Development: Alternatives for Program Implementation in the States,* because it calls for a vigorous role on the part of state agencies in the leadership for early childhood education.

THE IMPACT OF CULTURAL LAG ON EARLY CHILDHOOD EDUCATION

The theory of cultural lag developed by W. F. Ogburn in the 1920s is an intriguing idea in sociology. Ogburn defines it as a lag that occurs when two institutions or parts of the culture that have been correlated, experience change, causing less adjustment between them than existed previously. "Cultural lags are one characteristic of the process of social evolution which occurs in a closely integrated society in periods of rapid change."[12]

An application of the theory of cultural lag to aspects of early childhood education helps us to understand more clearly what is occurring within the educational enterprise. As programs for children under five years of age, such as Head-Start, have received wide public recognition, the role of the kindergarten as the one year, the initial experience, for educating young children seems too limited and narrow a definition for early childhood education. Here, then, is cultural lag. Kindergarten was correlated with the public education sequence as the year of experience children underwent before starting their formal education. The culture has undergone some sweeping changes in the past 25 years so that this no longer characterizes what is actually occurring in many parts of our society. "The emphasis on 'Kindergarten' and 'five-year-olds' is inconsistent with common developmental definitions of early childhood education which usually specify a broad range of about six chronological years, three through eight."[13]

Dr. Joe Frost clearly sets forth the causes of the cultural lag and its effects on early childhood education when he states:

> The myth that one single strand of philosophical, psychological, or educational theory is sufficient in itself to account for the complex develop-

12. William F. Ogburn, *On Culture and Social Change* (Chicago: University of Illinois Press, 1964), p. 95.
13. Joe L. Frost. "Early Childhood Development in Texas: A State in Need of Union," speech given at the Texas Early Childhood Conference, University of Houston, March 8, 1972, p. 3.

mental needs of all children has, throughout the history of American education, led to unfortunate consequences. The spectacular vision of Froebel and Dewey gave us the open school and child-centered learning. The child-based experiments of Montessori and Piaget made immeasurable contributions to developmental theory and practice. Maslow's studies of self-actualizing people focused our attention to the affective dimensions of the child and lent fuel to the free school movement within education. The dispassionate studies of Skinner viewed the child as animal but produced remarkable innovations in behavior modification . . .

The preoccupation with normative-based procedures—grade level standards, letter grades, promotion and retention schemes with roots in an outmoded "normative-maturational" view of learning, exemplifies a second educational myth. The "maturational" or "predeterministic" view that intelligence and potentiality are fixed at birth has given way to the more dynamic view that the abilities of the child are plastic and malleable by conditions of nurture, thus placing some responsibility upon adults as caretakers of their young.[14]

When viewed in a sociological perspective, early childhood education is suffering from cultural lag. The field is urgently in need of redefinition and re-evaluation so that a better "fit" will occur with other parts of the institution of education.

DYSFUNCTIONAL FORCES UPON EARLY CHILDHOOD ISSUES

We have mentioned the term "structural functionalism" several times. This refers to a school of sociologists whose approach to sociological theory advocated viewing the social system as made up of elements which formed a structure. These elements or parts functioned to maintain the balance or successful operation of the social system. Therefore the term "function" referred to a given activity that promoted the maintenance of the system.[15]

Social systems also encounter dysfunctional forces or dysfunctional events. Dysfunctions can be described as activities that interfere with the maintenance of the social system. An illustration of the dysfunctional process in early childhood education can be made when the issue of day care centers for young children of working mothers are attached to the Women's Liberation movement. The issue becomes even more embroiled when the day care center–women's rights' discussions take place on college campuses. The following quotation from the article "Metamorphosis of a Campus Radical" in the *New York Times Magazine* provides a firsthand example of dysfunctional activities that cause stress and strain on our social system.

14. Ibid., pp. 4–5.
15. Robert K. Merton, *Social Theory and Social Structure* (New York: Free Press Corporation, 1957).

Day care is thoroughly Women's Lib, a service to *free the university woman from the yoke of her children* [emphasis supplied]. There are five day-care centers serving students and faculty mothers at present [at the University of Iowa], and while their function is that of all-day kindergarten, their principles are those of the commune, breaking down the family pattern in favor of the community, of sexual freedom, and of the group taking the responsibility of loving and bringing up the children.

The pioneer day-care center, called Dum Dum, occupies a bare, university-owned house near the football stadium. When I called there a few weeks ago I found the two-year-olds toddling about, daubing each other with paint. Two men sat at a kitchen table, one doing water colors, the other comforting a child in his lap while a woman watched. A third man walked by with a plastic bag full of diapers. I was told that ordinarily the work is shared evenly between men and women. On the bulletin board I found some conventional messages: "Chris must have a nap—he may not go outside" and "Lane is missing a stocking hat." Below these was a notice that was distinctively day-care: "Men's group meets Monday evening . . . we are trying to raise our consciousness about sexism in general and deal with particularly offensive things we do as men."

Sitting in Dum Dum amid the toys and potties, one can't help thinking that the turning of all that inspired vandalism of yesteryear into this social service represents a painful comedown, and some observers say so—that day-care centers are an admission of impotence. Unable to make any dent on their elders, the radicals have turned to their kids in hopes of finding them more impressionable.[16]

Here we have a *male* writer, a novelist, describing college campus radicalism in 1972 by proposing his theory that sexism is the central issue in the university today. He characterizes the brave, daring, "big-man-on-campus" protestor of the 1960s as the diaper-carrying babysitter of the 1970s campus scene. He brings the day-care issue into the picture he is trying to paint of today's college man.

Dysfunctional forces thwart the work of early childhood educators who are diligently and honestly trying to present the causes of early education and the important contribution that men can make as teachers and role models for young children. When such descriptions of the male's activities in an early childhood program (*he* has a plastic pail full of diapers and *she* watches) are construed for the public, dysfunctions result.

The tools of the sociological method can provide us with the means for contesting such absurd assumptions that men are emasculated by day-care centers and that the family is being threatened if we provide group care for toddlers and preschoolers. We can ask what evidence can be presented to support such contentions. We can, in turn, produce studies and projects to verify the effectiveness of early educational experience. Soci-

16. John Legget, "Metamorphosis of the Campus Radical," *New York Times Magazine,* Jan. 30, 1972, pp. 19–20.

ology will help us demonstrate that day-care centers and other programs for young children are functions that promote the welfare of the social system and are not dysfunctional.

PROVIDING DYNAMIC LEADERS FOR THE FUTURE OF EARLY EDUCATION

One road to developing dynamic leaders in the field of early childhood education is to design training programs, workshops, and courses that stress the social scientific nature of the field. If we can place in the hands of those individuals who show promise and commitment in the teaching of young children, the social scientific information and knowledge we have just recently acquired on early growth and development, on effective techniques for teaching varying kinds of children, on developing curriculum and materials, a cadre of dynamic early educators could be produced. Sociology can make large contributions to the training of these leaders, in their effectiveness in working in smaller groups such as the classroom, with parents, administrators and colleagues; and in the larger, broader communities of the school district, the state, the region, the federal government arena; and finally in the world community of educators.

A Workshop: Leadership in Early Childhood Education with Emphasis upon Sociological Perspective. Currently, there are very few university programs offering advanced training in early childhood education. Yet a specific need can be cited for workshops, seminars, or conferences to offer experienced personnel insights and enrichment in the rapidly expanding field of early education. In the summer of 1971, the University of Denver held a five-week workshop titled, "Leadership in Early Childhood Education" for early childhood teachers, supervisors, and administrators, those working with children ages three through eight years. The workshop program included study in sociology, child psychology, intergroup relations, curriculum development, and early childhood education. The cultural arts, music, drama, and art were integrated through the program. Implications for supervision and administration of early childhood programs were stressed.

Activities in the workshop included:

reviewing resumes of research about the crucial nature of early learning;

developing theories and concepts in the social sciences by the use of literature, poetry, dramatization, and other language arts media;

use of music and art techniques, including demonstrations to foster a sense of ethnic pride and understanding of the contributions of various minorities;

compilation of early childhood curriculum materials and other published materials such as bibliographies, manuals, books, and games, including carrying out a search through the ERIC Early Childhood Education Clearinghouse;

study of the British infant school setting;

early diagnosis of learning disabilities in young children;

demonstrations of materials to present world perspectives to young children;

demonstrations of a wide range of early childhood curriculum materials from major educational firms;

lecture and demonstrations by Celia Stendler Lavatelli, University of Illinois, of her Piagetian curriculum materials;

lecture and media presentation by Oralie McAfee, University of Northern Colorado (New Nursery School), of her techniques, materials, and approach in early childhood education;

presentation of Man: A Course of Study (Educational Development Corporation) materials based on Jerome Bruner's theories with implications for young children;

development, presentation, and evaluation of curriculum designs, models, and projects appropriate for use in each participant's teaching or supervisory position, to be implemented in the 1971-72 school year.

Field trips included:

visit to the ERIC Clearinghouse on Social Science Education, Boulder, Colorado, for a session on how to use the ERIC system;

visit to the Title VI, Early Childhood Education van of the Denver Public Schools;

visit to the New Nursery School, Greeley, Colorado;

tour of the Samsonite Lego Plant, Loveland, Colorado, to observe the design, manufacture, and production of early childhood toys;

tour of the museums of Santa Fe, New Mexico, to see special exhibits on the costumery of the world;

attendance at the Santa Fe Opera Production of *The Magic Flute.*

Curriculum designs and materials developed by the participants of the Leadership in Early Childhood Education Workshop included projects like those described here.

Two curriculum designs that utilize the senses to learn about the world are titled "Who Am I?" and "I Am Here." These two designs use a socially-oriented approach for teaching both the cognitive and affective curriculum of five- and six-year-olds. The five senses form the springboard for teaching language arts, social studies, and mathematics concepts. The two early elementary school teachers who developed the project "I Am Here," state that their main objectives are to help the child realize that all our knowledge of the world comes to us through the senses.

> In preschool and kindergarten, children have the ability to formulate categories or classify. This classification first comes about through the basis of color of shape. This is frequently done with basic shapes of a square, circle, and triangle; the three primary colors, red, yellow, and blue. In introducing our unit on the senses, we have prepared charts, illustrations, statements, and questions starting with the basic shapes. These charts are called, "Discovering Your Senses Through Shapes and Color." Each of the senses is illustrated with a shape and (or) a color. Various objects familiar to the child are used to illustrate sight, hearing, taste, smell and feeling. The illustration is qualified by a statement clarifying the shape, followed by a sentence which shows this sense used in daily life. Each chart concludes with an open-ended question providing motivation for further discussion and discovery.
>
> In preparing these charts for our introduction to discovering the senses, we have selected content which takes the child from the known to the unknown; presenting first the visual concept, second the auditory concept, followed by all joining in verbalizing the concepts presented. This verbalizing should lead into the materials which we have accumulated and prepared for a four- or five-week study in our first grades. This would include a complete curriculum area for social studies, language arts, science and art and for this period of time. We have also reviewed the complete filmstrips with sound records called, "Discovering Your Senses" published by Coronet Films, Inc. We found they contained excellent material to implement the study of the senses.[17]

Another sociologically-oriented approach to using the senses as a basis for the early childhood curriculum was formulated by Susan Boner, a kindergarten teacher in Colorado. Mrs. Boner writes:

> As a kindergarten teacher, a goal that I feel takes top priority in my teaching is to help each child to become more aware of himself as an individual. In this over-populated and shrinking world of ours where the words "identity crisis" are being heard more and more each day, I think that it is very important for the child in the early stages of his development to begin to think about who he is and what it means to be human in order to prepare him for the adjustments that he will have to make in his future. When the children leave me in the spring, I want each one to walk out of kindergarten with the feeling that "I count, I am worthwhile, and I have a big contribution to make to this world."
>
> How can we, as teachers, help a child to get to know himself? In this paper, I have tried to answer this question. I hope that the ideas presented here will give you new insight into the important task of developing and deepening self-awareness in kindergarten children.[18]

17. Phyllis Clark and Fanchon Bosma. "I Am Here," mimeographed project for Workshop: Leadership in Early Childhood Education, School of Education, University of Denver, summer 1971, pp. 3–4.

18. Susan Boner. "Who Am I?" mimeographed project for Workshop: Leadership in Early Childhood Education, School of Education, University of Denver, summer 1971.

The paper then presents materials, ideas, and activities under the categories of "My Physical Self," "My Emotions," "My Five Senses," "My Social Self." (See Appendix B for bibliographic references on these topics.)

These three teachers prepared their curriculum designs for specific teaching assignments. They returned to their classrooms in the fall of 1971 and proceeded to implement the designs and use the materials they had outlined during the summer workshop. In conversations with these teachers during the 1971-72 school year, they each reported how valuable and worthwhile they found the effort and energy expended the previous summer in putting together their curriculum designs. They praised the social scientific approach as powerful tools in helping them to develop meaningful programs for their young students.

Reorganizing a Head Start Center. Here is another example of how a participant in the Leadership in Early Childhood Education Workshop planned, organized and put into written form a curriculum guide built upon social scientific theory for her early childhood program. This participant is the head teacher in a Head-Start Center. Her attempt to express in writing the philosophy and background for this planned change in the total organization of the Head Start Center is particularly noteworthy. The scholarship and acumen that she displayed in this effort makes it appropriate for presentation here almost in its entirety as an example of what we mean by leadership qualities in early childhood education.

CURRICULUM GUIDE FOR A HEAD START CENTER

Introduction. I would like to create a curriculum guide for my personal use, outlining the kind of educational program I feel is needed by Westwood Head Start children; and one I would like to conduct and could conduct in my present setting. This guide would be for three months duration. It would make use of the suggested curriculum guides now available to Head Start teachers, but up until now these curriculum guides have not been correlated for use with each other. The educational philosophy in my program would be based on a blending of my personal philosophy, which emphasized affective learning because of my religious education background and my Head Start training and experience. Mainly, though, the basis of the program would stem from the "Five Point Affective and Cognitive Objectives" described in the *The New Nursery School* (G. Nimnicht, O. McAfee, J. Meier, General Learning Corp., 1970).

New experiences and knowledge should initiate new dimensions of growth in a person, as well as in a society or a school system. I am trying to respond to many forces that have shaped me into the person that I am. I cannot accept any one specific approach as outlined by the various experts. I see merit in some aspects of all of them and realize I use Piagetian theory, Montessori-type toys, and find Deutsch's studies

Fig. 5.2, 5.3. Self-portraits, University Park Elementary School Kindergarten, Denver, Colorado.

most helpful in working with the culturally deprived child. I modify behavior and give much opportunity for individual learning, as in the British Infant Schools. I put much emphasis in meeting the psychological needs of the child, as Erikson and Bettleheim would advocate.

I believe that this is not a cop-out, but proof of some flexibility and a recognition that different approaches are not only valid but necessary. I know that some children learn best in one or two ways; that most children learn best through a variety of ways; that different types of subject matter and/or goals are learned best in seemingly opposite ways; and that intellectual, social, psychological, and physical growth cannot be experienced through any one procedure. It is the whole child that the preschool teacher—especially Head Start teachers—lives and works with.

My goals for the child would be to help him develop his full potential—emotionally, psychologically, socially, intellectually, and physically. To do this I would try to allow for as much creativity as possible—and as much conformity as necessary; as much "Chicano" as possible—as much "Anglo" as necessary; as free as possible and as structured as necessary. The decisions as to "how much" in either direction is constantly being determined by: (a) my knowledge of the characteristics of the preschool child; (b) my knowledge, appreciation, and understanding of the individual child—his background, potential, abilities and disabilities and personality; (c) my goals for the classroom; and (d) my own personality and values.[19]

This Head Start teacher then developed in detail the changes in her program she would be attempting during the coming school year. This included changes in the organization for use of paraprofessionals and assistants in her Center, changes in the curriculum content, a detailed plan called the "Special Five Time" for science and mathematics activities, musical activities, and creative dramatics. She also drew up a time schedule, week by week, detailing daily schedules for the program content with specific activities and materials listed for each day of each week. This carefully organized planning has made it possible for her to make the most optimum use of assistants, paraprofessionals, and parents in her Head Start Center, as well as the college students from the Early Childhood Education courses that this writer has assigned to the Head Start program at the Westwood Center.

A Specialized Early Childhood Program. One participant in the Workshop was a teacher in a unique and innovative early childhood program developed by the Denver Public Schools. Growing out of a proposal during the 1968-69 school year the Early Childhood Primary Education Committee of the Denver Schools established three early childhood programs serving four-year-olds in disadvantaged, target areas of Denver. In

---

19. Elizabeth Goding, "Developing a Curriculum Guide for a Head Start Program," mimeographed project for Workshop: Leadership in Early Childhood Education, School of Education, University of Denver, summer 1971, pp. 2–6.

1971 two more such programs were established, with hopes of opening others as funds became available. It seemed appropriate to develop a brochure for parents describing and explaining the Early Childhood Education Centers of the Denver Public Schools. So as her project for the Leadership in Early Childhood Education Workshop, Charlotte Rubin wrote and illustrated an attractive 20-page pamphlet on the program. Mrs. Rubin's understanding of sociological concepts and theories relating to the family, to ethnic affiliations, to intergroup relations, and to the culture of the school were definite assets in planning and writing the pamphlet.

These projects from the advanced graduate level course in early childhood education, Leadership in Early Childhood Education, demonstrate how multi-disciplinary, social science perspectives with emphasis on planning and coordination can provide early childhood personnel with the framework to develop sound, meaningful, and workable curricula and classroom organizations for effective teaching. The projects reflect a number of theoretical positions and approaches in early education. All the work is grounded in theory and research, yet shaped by the years of practical experience these teachers have had in working with young children in early childhood education programs.

AN INTRODUCTORY COURSE FOR EARLY CHILDHOOD EDUCATION WITH SOCIOLOGICAL ORIENTATION

As the early childhood education field receives more publicity and attention, college students enrolled in conventional education departments and schools of education preparing for careers in elementary education have been asking for courses specializing in the teaching of the younger child, ages four to seven years. To meet this need, some education departments are offering courses titled "early childhood education" within their elementary education sequences. The content of these college offerings are wide-ranging and highly variable. Here is an example of one such undergraduate-level course in early childhood education with a sociological orientation offered to upper-level (juniors and seniors) education majors who have prerequisite courses in Educational Psychology and Introduction to Elementary Education.

> *Objectives of the course*
> to introduce the student to the new and rapidly expanding educational frontier, early childhood education;
> to present some of the vast array of models, designs, programs now ongoing in early childhood education;
> to survey the impact of research in early childhood on curriculum, programming, and methodology;

to examine the crucial role of socioeconomic level, ethnicity, and family influences in early childhood education;
to view with a sociological perspective some future trends and directions in early childhood education.

The early childhood education students meet twice a week on the college campus to discuss readings, see films and demonstrations, exchange ideas. One day or more a week they spend working on early childhood programs—Head Start Centers, private nursery schools, public school kindergartens. In this way the students can combine theory with practice. Further, they can have an experience in working with young children to find out if they really wish to pursue a career in early childhood education. Whenever possible the early childhood education students are placed with the experienced teachers who have participated in an advanced early childhood course, such as the Leadership in Early Childhood Education Workshop, offered at alternate times on a graduate level. This practice reinforces the interdisciplinary approach that stresses sociological, as well as phychological and cognitive development factors in working with young children.

As the culmination of the early childhood education course, the students participate in an oral examination. In groups of three or four they meet with the instructor for about one hour to discuss topics and questions that have arisen from the content and activities of the course. These discussions center around issues such as the importance of working with the child in his sociocultural environment; meeting the needs of teaching young children in a pluralistic society; why one should study the community and neighborhood in which your students live; delineating some of the characteristics of dysfunctional behavior; describing how social class and ethnic affiliation are manifest in behavior; describing how children learn the norms, values, roles, and status positions of their group and in the broader society; and questioning if social interaction between children of different ethnic groups tends to really reduce stereotyping and prejudice.

In the undergraduate level course in early childhood education, as in the advanced seminar, the complexity of the field, with its inputs from the various social science disciplines, education, and the humanities, is presented. Students are informed of the political aspects, economic and social implications of early childhood education. Far from being an "Introduction to Babysitting 1," this Early Childhood Education course poses strenuous obligations upon the students who elect it.

A PRE-CONVENTION CLINIC AT A NATIONAL CONFERENCE

Another road providing early childhood enthusiasts the opportunity to influence other educators and inform them of the importance of early childhood education is that of inclusion of the topic or area at national educational conventions and conferences. For example, during the 1971 National Council for the Social Studies Meeting in Denver, Colorado, a pre-convention clinic of two days duration titled "Social Studies in the Early Childhood Curriculum" was offered. The program considered the following topics on the sociology of early childhood education in four working groups that functioned in the informal open session style of the British Primary School: stereotypes, myths, attitudes, and values in the social studies programs of young children; viewing the school and the classroom as a community; a world perspective in the early childhood classroom; teaching young children about social conflict and social problems. A wide range of exemplary materials in the social education of young children were displayed as part of the clinic, and participants surveyed and examined these materials for consideration of use in their programs. They also previewed multimedia materials, made demonstration art projects, and toured the newly opened Denver Art Museum's displays of folk art and fine art.

This was the first time the National Council for the Social Studies had included on the program a special pre-convention clinic that focused on social studies materials for children ages four to eight years. The clinic was very well attended by social studies supervisors, both elementary and secondary levels, teachers, curriculum coordinators, administrators, university faculty, and textbook and media producers and writers. The burgeoning of interest in early education has caught many supervisors, administrators, textbook and curriculum materials publishers unprepared and with limited knowledge about the field. Having clinics, workshops and seminars at regional and national conferences of major education associations will help to disseminate the new knowledge and research about teaching young children. Further, it will alert educators to the importance of the sociological perspective in early childhood education in the total spectrum of the educational enterprise.

SOME SUGGESTIONS FOR MORE OPTIMUM TRAINING PROGRAMS IN EARLY CHILDHOOD EDUCATION

We have been describing programs in the training of early childhood education that are more or less ancillary and auxiliary in nature. If we are to recognize early education as an integral part of the educational enterprise, then we must develop full scale and fully accredited higher education programs including masters and doctoral degrees in the area. Particularly for the requirements in advanced degrees in early childhood education, sociology, as well as social psychology and anthropology, should be included in the preparation of masters and doctoral candidates. The degree of Master of Arts in Early Childhood Education and Doctor of Education in Early Childhood should carry interdisciplinary connotations which include the social sciences and the humanities, as well as in-depth background in child psychology and education with emphasis on learning theory. This type of preparation for advanced degrees in early childhood education, therefore, calls for humanistic and social scientific backgrounds rather than the more traditional preparation in home economics departments or in family living curricula of public and private universities.

Another suggestion that we would urge and underscore is the bringing of worldwide programs into early childhood education in the form of distinct courses of study such as comparative early childhood education. This could include exchanges, opportunities for student teaching in other countries around the globe, and/or working in early childhood centers or programs in other nations. The great concern and interest in young children that societies everywhere have expressed in recent years make it possible to consider a variety of worldwide early childhood programs beyond mere visitations to British infant schools, or Danish playgrounds, Israeli kibbutz, or Soviet "detsky sad." Now we have a growing body of literature on early childhood centers around the world, as well as cross-cultural comparisons in child-rearing and socialization. Such offerings should become a requirement in both graduate and undergraduate programs in early childhood education.

One Last Look. In this final chapter we have summarized the uses of sociology for early childhood education. Sociological views of power were examined for their implications in early childhood education at the federal and at the state level of governmental support. The theory of cultural lag was applied to early childhood education as was the concept of dysfunctional events upon the field. Finally, programs with a sociological focus for developing dynamic leaders for early childhood education were presented. This included some examples of the type of projects and planning that can be created through social scientific, humanistically-based higher education and training.

This book was conceived with the hope that sociological theory can prove useful to those working with young children to enable them to gain stature and greater effectiveness in following their chosen careers. In closing let us repeat what young children everywhere say to their teachers as they arrive at school, "Tee-chur, I'm *here!*" Then let us acknowledge the great challenge and the equally great rewards there are in being a teacher of young children.

Fig. 5.4. Self-portrait, University Park Elementary School Kindergarten, Denver, Colorado.

Sources

Boocock, Sarane Spence. *An Introduction to the Sociology of Learning.* Boston: Houghton Mifflin Co., 1972.

Cuzzort, R. P. *Humanity and Modern Sociological Thought.* New York: Holt, Rinehart & Winston, Inc., 1969.

Education Commission of the States, Task Force on Early Childhood Education. *Early Childhood Development: Alternatives for Program Implementation in the States.* Denver, Colorado, 1971.

Frost, Joe L., ed. *Early Childhood Education Rediscovered.* New York: Holt, Rinehart & Winston, Inc., 1968.

Hunter, Elizabeth. *Encounter in the Classroom: New Ways of Teaching.* New York: Holt, Rinehart & Winston, Inc., 1972.

Lavatelli, Celia Stendler. *Piaget's Theory Applied to an Early Childhood Curriculum.* Boston: American Science and Engineering, 1970.

Mountainview Center for Environmental Studies. *Outlook,* no. 4, Winter 1971. Boulder, Colorado.

Resources and Materials
for Developing Worldmindedness
in the Kindergarten

Prepared by Carolyn Dungan
Denver Public Schools

Books for Teachers

Dittman, Laura, ed. *Curriculum Is What Happens: Planning Is the Key*. Washington, D.C.: National Association for the Education of Young Children, 1970, $1.75.

This booklet is designed to help teachers plan a meaningful curriculum for all areas of the school program.

Griffin, Louise, comp. *Books in Pre-School*. ERIC-NAEYC Publication in Early Childhood Education. Washington, D.C.: National Association for the Education of Young Children, 1970.

This booklet is a guide to selecting, purchasing, and using children's books. Included in the annotated bibliography are books about minority group children and bilingual books. A list of foreign book importers and U.S. book wholesalers is also included.

Griffin, Louise, comp. *Multi-ethnic Books for Young Children*. ERIC-NAEYC Publication in Early Childhood Education. Washington, D.C.: National Association for the Education of Young Children, 1970, $2.00.

An excellent annotated bibliography of multi-ethnic books for young children. The bibliography is indexed according to ethnic emphasis, with suggested appropriate age designations for each entry.

King, Edith. *The World: Context for Teaching in the Elementary School*. Dubuque, Ia.: Wm. C. Brown Co., Publishers, 1971, $3.95.

This book provides an introduction to the concept of "worldmindedness" and a basic framework for teaching this concept in the elementary school. The book also lists materials suitable for use with young children.

Miel, Alice. *The Shortchanged Children of Suburbia: What the Schools Don't Teach About Human Differences and What Can be Done About It*. New York: Institute of Human Relations Press, 1967, 95¢.

A summary report of a four-year study of how suburban children are taught to live in a multicultural society. A "must" background reading for teachers

157

in order to avoid a superficial, "quaint customs" approach to cultural differences.

Taylor, Harold. *The World as Teacher.* Garden City, New York: Doubleday & Co., Inc., 1969.

This book is concerned with teacher education and expansion of the concept of a "world society."

Multi-Media Materials

Bowmar Early Childhood Series. Glendale, Calif.: Bowmar, 1967.

The series includes multi-ethnic books with simple text and color photographs of experiences familiar to young children in a modern urban community, recordings of the stories, and large picture story sets. Books, records, and pictures may be purchased separately.

Jarolimek, John, and Davis, Bertha. Social Studies Focus on Active Learning Series. New York: The Macmillan Co., 1971.
Level 1: Zolotow, Charlotte. *You and Me* and *Here We Are.*

This excellent book with simple text and beautiful colored illustrations is the first book in this multimedia system. The book, divided into four parts—Your Family, Their Families, Places, Me and You—is designed to help young children discover the commonalities and differences across a country and across the world. Children can begin to understand that where one lives determines how he lives.

The complete multimedia system includes the text, work sheets, sort cards, films, large display cards, overhead transparencies, records, and teacher's guide for coordinated use of all media.

King, Edith. *Discovering the World.* New Rochelle, New York: Spoken Arts, Inc., 1970, $60.

An unusual multi-media program including four color filmstrips, accompanying recordings, and a teacher's guide, "designed to sensitize young children to the universality of the human condition, and to awareness of the needs and ways of others." Parts I and II, The Universal Language of Children, help young children discover through music and art that children all around the world "are experiencing, feeling, needing, THEIR places, THEIR parents, THEIR people, THEIR pets." Part III, Cultural Dignity, helps young children understand that wherever people live they create "things of beauty." Through art, "boys and girls can learn to enjoy space, line, texture, color, design, and form." Part IV, Masks, traces the origins of masks to primitive man. Young children are helped to discover the kinds of masks used throughout the world.

MATCH: Multi-sensory Learning Units for Social Studies, The City
Boston: American Science and Engineering.

The City Unit is designed for Kindergarten through Grade 3 to help young children understand "what a city is, what happens in it, how it changes." Materials include books, photographs, record, film, wooden buildings, and a teacher's guide so children can be involved in building a city, and solving problems related to city living.

Pictures That Teach Morristown, N.J.: Silver Burdett Co.

The Earth, Home of People	10-181-6, 1966
The Families Around the World:	
Living in the U.S.	10-181-5-315, 1967
Living in Kenya	10-181-3-313, 1966
Living in Japan	10-181-1-311, 1966
Living in Brazil	10-181-4-314, 1967
Living in France	
Living in the Soviet Union	10-281-7, 1970
Living in Mexico	10-281-12, 1970
Christmas Around the World	10-182-2-317, 1966

Each set contains large colored photographs to stimulate role playing and group discussion of life around the world.

Senesh, Lawrence. *Our Working World: Families at Work, Neighbors at Work, Cities at Work.* Chicago: Science Research Associates, Inc., 1964.

This Social Studies Program for grades 1-3 is based on children's experiences and their relation to the fundamental principles of economic knowledge. The program includes records, filmstrips, textbooks, activity books for children, and teacher's resource units with related stories, poems, records, songs, films, and filmstrips, textbooks, activity books for children, and teacher's resource units with related stories, poems, records, songs, films, and filmstrips listed. Although the series is designed for grades 1-3, the teacher's Resource Units are excellent sources of materials appropriate for use with kindergarten children.

Shaftel, Fannie, and Shaftel, George. *Words and Action: Role-Playing Photo-Problems for Young Children.* New York: Holt, Rinehart & Winston, Inc., 1967.

An excellent series of large black and white photographs designed to stimulate verbal and action responses from young children in social conflict situations. The photographs include black and white children in the city and school environment.

Music

Dietz, Betty and Park, Thomas, eds. *Folk Songs of China, Japan, Korea.* New York: The John Day Co., Inc., 1964.

A collection of folk songs from China, Japan, and Korea in English and native language accompanied by a limited selection of recorded songs.

Kaufman, William *UNICEF Book of Children's Songs.* Harrisburg, Pa.: Stackpole Books, 1970.

A collection of folk songs and photographs of children throughout the world to help young children move over the barriers of language through music to understand cultures around the world.

Jaye, Mary. *Making Music Your Own.* Kindergarten. Morristown, N.J.: Silver Burdette Co., 1971.

This basic music text with beautiful multi-ethnic colored illustrations, poetry, and accompanying recordings of each song in the text includes many lovely folk songs from around the world.

Maynes, J. O., comp. *Cancionoro Alegro.* Arizona State Department of Public Instruction, 1968.
A compilation of Spanish songs in the Spanish language, including Spanish Christmas songs.

McCall, Adeline. *This Is Music for Kindergarten and Nursery School.* Boston: Allyn & Bacon, Inc., 1967.
This basic music text includes Eskimo and Indian songs and American folk songs.

Rodgers, Richard, and Hammerstein, Oscar. Songs from *The King and I.* "Getting to Know You", "I Whistle a Happy Tune," and "The March of Siamese Children." New York: Williamson Music, Inc., 1956.

Rodgers, Richard, and Hammerstein, Oscar. Songs from *The Sound of Music.* "Do-Re-Mi" and "Edelweiss." New York: Williamson Music, Inc., 1959.

Sherman, Richard, and Sherman, Robert. "It's a Small World." Glendale: Wonderland Music Company, Inc., 1963, 75¢.

Songs Children Like: Folk Songs from Many Lands. Washington, D.C.: Association for Childhood Education International, 1958, 75¢.
An excellent collection of folk songs children enjoy from many countries.

Sur, William *et al. This Is Music, Book I.* Boston: Allyn & Bacon, Inc., 1966.
A basic music text including a section of foreign language songs.

Watters, Lorrain *et al. The Magic of Music, Book Two.* Boston: Ginn and Co., 1966.
Included in this book are many folk songs related to developing world-mindedness that are appropriate for kindergarten children.

Wolfe, Irving; Krone, Beatrice; and Fullerton, Margaret. *Voices of the World.* Together-We-Sing Series. Chicago: Follett Publishing Co., 1960.
A spiral-bound collection of songs from many lands: Canada, the British Isles, Scandinavia, the Low Countries, Western Europe, Spain and Italy, Eastern Europe, the Near East, Africa, Asia, Australia, the Pacific Islands, Latin America, the United States. Included are suggestions for rhythmic activities and dance, and related recordings and readings.

Dance

Books

Kulbitsky, Olga and Kaltman, Frank. *Teacher's Dance Handbook, No. I, Kindergarten to Sixth Grade.* Newark, N. J.: Bluebird Publishing Co., 1959.
This book presents an integrated folkdance program coordinated with Folkraft Records.

La Salle, Dorothy. *Rhythms and Dance for Elementary Schools.* New York: The Ronald Press Co., 1951.
Contents include fundamental dance movements, simple folk dances from around the world, and singing games.

Records

Bowmar Records, Glendale, California:

Singing Games and Folk Dances, #3 (games and folk dances from other countries), #112, $5.95.

Folk Dances #4 (dances from around the world), #113, $5.95.

Folk Dances #5 (American), #114, $5.95.

Folk Dances #6 (Latin-American), #115, $5.95.

Dances of Hawaii (ancient and modern), #116, $5.95.

Mexican Folk Dances, #117, $5.95.

Canadian Folk Dances, #118, $5.95.

Folkraft Records:

#1184, Let Your Feet Go Tap (German)

#1187 Danish Dance of Greeting

#1119 La Raspa (Mexican Hat Dance)

Russell Records, Ventura, California:

#33-725, Chimes of Dunkirk, Jump Jim Crow, How D'Ye Do My Partner, A Hunting We Will Go

#33-750, Seven Steps, Shoemaker's Dance, Children Polka, Klappdans

United States Committee for UNICEF, United Nations, New York:

Hi Neighbor, Record 2—songs and dances from Brazil, Ghana, Israel, Japan, Turkey

Hi Neighbor, Record 3—songs and dances from Chile, Greece, Ethiopia, Nigeria, Thailand

Games

McWhirter, Mary, ed. *Games Enjoyed by Children Around the World.* American Friends Service Committee, Inc., 160 N. 15th Street, Philadelphia, Pa. 19102, 50¢.

A booklet of 50 games played around the world to help children identify with boys and girls of other cultures and to realize the universality of play materials and games.

Bowman Records:

Singing Games #1, #110, $5,95.

Singing Games #2, #111, $5.95.

Recordings

Halina't Umwit, Mahuhay Singers, Philippine sing-a-long tunes

MLP-5048, Villar Records, Mareco, Inc., 131 Del Monte Avenue, Quezon City, Philippines

It's A Small World

ST 3925, A Disneyland Record

Music of the World's Peoples, Volume 2, FE 4505

Folkways Records, 701 7th Avenue, New York, N.Y.

Music from Cuba, Finland, Ukraine, Canada, American Sioux Indians,

Serbia, China, Italy, Iran, Austrailian Aborigines, Chile, Albania, Western Congo, Jewish, Kashmir, Azerbaijan.

Taos Recordings and Publications, Taos, New Mexico
    TRP 1, Taos Indian Songs with Pete Concha
    TRP-7, More Taos Indian Songs, with Pete and Isabel Concha

This Is Rhythm, Ella Jenkins
    Folkways Records FC 7652
    An introduction to rhythm using rhythm instruments including bongos, sticks, maracas, guiro, cow bell, and wood block.

Art

Baylor, Byrd. Illus. Bahti, Tom. *Before You Came This Way.* New York: E. P. Dutton and Co., Inc., 1969, $4.75.
    This book contains beautiful bronze-tone bark paper illustrations of pre-historic Indian petroglyphs on canyon walls and cliff dwellings in the American Southwest. The drawings are accompanied by the story of early man and discussion of his simple art form.

Coe, Michael. *America's First Civilization: Discussing the Olmec.* New York: American Heritage Publishing Co., Inc., 1968.
    Excellent background reading for the teacher for introducing art and architecture of the Middle American cultures to young children. Many color and black and white photographs are included which are appropriate for young children.

Cultural Arts Program, Denver Public Schools.
    Files list resource artists available in the Denver area and appropriate field trips for students.

Glubok, Shirley. *The Art of Africa.* New York: Harper & Row, Publishers, 1965.
    Black and white photographs with accompanying text to illustrate African art—sculpture, masks, reliefs, heads, paintings, statues, baskets, pottery.

Raboff, Ernest. *Paul Klee: Art for Children.* Ed. by Bradley Smith. Garden City, N. Y.: Doubleday & Co., Inc., 1968, $3.95.
    The story of Paul Klee, a Swiss artist who states that "Art does not re-produce the visible. It renders it visible." "In this way we learn to look beyond the surface and get to the roots of things." Color and black-and-white reproductions of Klee's work indicate a delightful use of color and line appealing to young children.

History and Customs

Indian and Eskimo Children. Washington, D.C.: United States Department of the Interior, Bureau of Indian Affairs, 35¢.
    Photographs and simple text explaining how Indians and Eskimos live, and their contributions to the United States.

Marcus, Rebecca. *The First Book of Cliff Dwellings*. New York: Franklin Watts, Inc., 1969.

This book contains photographs and simple descriptions of many cliff dwellings in the American Southwest.

Price, Christine. *Happy Days*. A UNICEF Book of Birthdays, Name Days and Growing Days. New York: United States Committee for UNICEF, United Nations, 1969, $3.00.

Excellent background reading for teachers emphasizing the importance of the child to his family and various customs throughout the world. Includes full-page color prints of scenes around the world, music of birthday songs from other countries, naming children around the world, and a brief bibliography.

Spiegelman, Judith. *UNICEF's Festival Book*. New York: United States Committee for UNICEF, United Nations, 1966, $2.00.

Full-page color drawings and accompanying one-page text explaining holidays celebrated in different parts of the world.

The Indians of New Mexico: Apache, Navajo, Pueblo, Ute. Santa Fe: Museum of New Mexico Press, 1963, 50¢.

Background reading for teachers along with drawings suitable for young children illustrating the contributions of the Indians of New Mexico.

The Mesa Verde Story. Diorama Series, Mesa Verde National Park Museum.

A series of color reproductions of five dioramas located at the Mesa Verde National Park Museum, with accompanying background data for each diorama.

Watson, Don. *Cliff Dwellings of the Mesa Verde: A Story in Pictures*. Mesa Verde Museum Association, Mesa Verde National Park, Colorado.

Black and white photographs and historical account of Mesa Verde.

Poetry

Kaufman, William. *UNICEF Book of Children's Poems*. Harrisburg, Pa.: Stackpole Books, 1970.

A collection of poems expressing the feeling and thoughts of boys and girls around the world with accompanying black and white photographs.

Kaufman, William. *UNICEF Book of Children's Prayers*. Harrisburg, Pa.: Stackpole Books, 1970.

A collection of prayers and black-and-white photographs from around the world to help children understand the feelings of children in other lands for their God.

Scott, Louise and Thompson, J. J. *Rhymes for Fingers and Flannelboards*. New York: Webster Division-McGraw-Hill, 1960, $5.25.

This excellent collection of fingerplays and rhymes includes a section of rhymes from other lands.

Literature

Amescua, Carol. *The Story of Pablo, Mexican Boy*. Chicago: Encyclopedia Britannica Press, 1952, $1.00.

The true-to-life story of Pablo is accompanied by excellent color photographs.

Ayer, Jacqueline. *The Paper-Flower Tree*. A Tale from Thailand. New York: Harcourt, Brace Jovanovich, Inc., 1962.

The story of a Thailand girl and her faith that she could grow a paper-flower tree.

Beim, Lorraine and Beim, Jerrold. *Two Is a Team*. New York: Harcourt, Brace Jovanovich, Inc., 1945, $2.75.

A white and black boy work together to solve a problem.

Bemelmans, Ludwig. *Madeline*. New York: Simon and Schuster, 1939.

The story of Madeline, a little French girl, and her stay in the hospital.

Bishop, Claire. *Five Chinese Brothers*. New York: Coward-McCann, Inc., 1938.

A favorite Chinese folk tale.

Coatsworth, Elizabeth. *The Children Come Running*. New York: Golden Press, 1960.

A collection of poems, stories, and color art reproductions of children around the world.

Crowder, Jack L. *Stephannie and the Coyote*. Box 278, Bernalillo, New Mexico, 87004, 1969.

Full-page color photographs and story of a seven-year-old Navajo Indian girl. Story written in English and Navajo.

Ets, Marie Hall. *Gilberto and the Wind*. New York: Viking Press, 1963.

A charming story and drawings of a little Mexican boy and his playmate—the wind.

—————————. *Play With Me*. New York: Viking Press, 1955.

The story of an Anglo girl and her search for someone to play with.

—————————, and Labastida, Aurora. *Nine Days to Christmas*. New York: Viking Press, 1959.

The story of a Mexican kindergarten girl and her first Christmas posada. The story describes the festive posada and breaking the pinata.

Fader, Shirley. "The Boy Who Was Fussy About His Friends." *American Junior Red Cross News,* November, 1966.

Flack, Marjorie. *The Story About Ping*. New York: Viking Press, 1933.

An old favorite of a duck who lives on the Yangtze River in China.

Francoise. *Springtime for Jeanne-Marie*. New York: Charles Scribner's Sons, 1955.

The story of a little French girl's search for her lost pet duck.

Grifalconi, Ann. *City Rhythms*. New York: Bobbs-Merrill Co., Inc., 1965.

A black boy becomes aware of the sounds of the city.

Handforth, Thomas. *Mei Li*. Garden City: Doubleday & Co., 1938, $3.50.
This Caldecott award book tells the story of little girls in China.

Keats, Ezra Jack. *Goggles!* New York: The Macmillan Co., 1969.
A delightful story of how two urban black boys worked together to solve a problem.

——————. *Whistle for Willie*. New York: Viking Press, 1964, $3.50.
A little black boy learns to whistle for his dog.

Matsuno, Masako. *A Pair of Red Clogs*. Cleveland: World Publishing Co., 1960, $3.50.
The story of a little Japanese girl who cracks her new red clogs.

Maxwell, Moreau. *Eskimo Family*. Chicago: Encyclopedia Britannica Press, 1962, $1.00.
A true-to-life story of an Eskimo family with color photographs.

Politi, Leo. *Rosa*. New York: Charles Scribner's Sons, 1963, $3.25.
A picture story of a Mexican girl.

Rose, Ronald. *Ngari, The Hunter*. New York: Harcourt Brace Jovanovich, Inc., 1968, $3.95.
The story of a young aboriginal boy who lives in the arid desert of central Australia. Color photographs are included.

Sakade, Florence, ed. *Urashima Taro and Other Japanese Children's Stories*. Rutland, Vermont: Charles T. Tuttle Co., 1961.
A collection of ten Japanese stories and illustrations to give Western children "a sense of identity with Japanese children and also explain some of the different customs."

Sharpe, Stella. *Tobo*. Chapel Hill: University of North Carolina Press, 1939, $3.00.
The story of a Negro farm boy in North Carolina.

Udry, Janice May. *What Mary Jo Shared*. Chicago: Albert Whitman & Co., 1966.
A delightful story of the surprise a little black girl brought to kindergarten for Sharing Time.

Resources and Materials
for Project "Who Am I?"

Prepared by Susan Boner
Brighton, Colorado Public Schools

My Physical Self

Books

Bannon, Laura. *The Best House in the World*. Boston: Houghton Mifflin Co., 1952, $2.25.

Golden, Augusta. *Straight Hair, Curly Hair*. New York: Thomas Y. Crowell Co., 1966, $2.96.

Lerner, Marguerite. *Red Man, White Man, African Chief*. Minneapolis, Minnesota: Lerner Publications Co. (Medical Books for Children), 1968, $3.95. All About Me—a set of books.

Selsam, Millicent. *All Kinds of Babies and How They Grow*. New York: William R. Scott, Inc., 1953, $2.00.

Showers, Paul. *How You Talk*. New York: Thomas Y. Crowell Co., 1962, $2.96.

Showers, Paul. *How Many Teeth?* New York: Thomas Y. Crowell Co., 1966, $3.50.

Showers, Paul. *Look at Your Eyes*. New York: Thomas Y. Crowell Co., 1962, $3.50.

Stenek, Muriel. *I Can Do It*. Chicago: Benefic Press, 1967, $1.20.

Films

Coronet Films, Coronet Building, 65 East South Water Street, Chicago, Illinois 60601.

Alexander Learns Good Health
How Billy Keeps Clean
John Avoids a Cold

My Emotions

Books

Ardizzone, Edward. *Tim All Alone*. New York: Henry Z. Walck Inc., 1957.

Crossen, Stacy J. and Natalie Covell. *Me is How I Feel*. (Poems) New York: McCall Publishing Co., 1970.

Krauss, Ruth. *The Happy Day*. New York: Harper & Row, 1970.

Ojemann, Ralph H. *Crying Again*. Cleveland: Educational Research Council, 1966.

Ormsby, Virginia. *What's Wrong With Julie?* Philadelphia, Pa.: J. B. Lippincott Co., 1965.

Rosenberg, Ethel. *Your Face Is A Picture.* Indianapolis: E. C. Seale and Co., Inc., 1963, $2.80.

Schultz, Charles M. *Happiness Is.* . . . San Francisco, Calif.: Determined Productions, Inc., 1967.

Schultz, Charles M. *Happiness Is a Warm Puppy.* San Francisco, Calif.: Determined Productions, Inc., 1968.

Schultz, Charles M. *Happiness is a Sad Song.* San Francisco, Calif.: Determined Productions, Inc., 1969.

Sonneborn, Ruth A. *The Lollipop Party.* New York: The Viking Press, 1967.

Films

Our Angry Feelings. Northfield, Illinois: Newenhouse Corp. (16mm)

This film shows how frustration, injustice, and bruised ego arouses angry feelings; what the effects of anger are; and how we can resolve angry actions and feelings.

What to Do About Upset Feelings. Chicago: Coronet. (16mm)

Circle of Feelings. This is an excellent film put out by SRA in their Focus on Self Development materials for kindergarten. It describes Sigh Sadness, Ha Ha Happiness, Gurrr Anger, and Trembly Fear and describes different incidents that have caused these displays of feelings.

My Five Senses

Books

Anderson, Hans Christian. *The Emperor's New Clothes.* Boston: Houghton Mifflin Co., 1949.

Borton, Helen. *Do You Hear What I Hear?* London: Abelard-Schuman, 1960.

Brandenberg, Aliki. *My Five Senses.* New York: Thomas Y. Crowell Co., 1962.

Bridwell, Norman. *The Big Red Dog.* New York: Scholastic Book Service, 1966.

Brown, Georgiana. *Look and See.* Chicago: Milment Publishing, Inc., 1958.

Budney, Blossom. *A Kiss is Round.* New York: Lothrop, 1954.

Donovan, John. *The Little Orange Book.* New York: William Morrow and Co., 1961.

Elkin, Ben. *The Loudest Noise in the World.* New York: Viking Press, 1954.

Erickson, Mary. *About Glasses for Gladys.* Chicago: Melmont Pub., 1962.

Holl, Adelaide. *Colors are Nice.* New York: Golden Press, 1962.

O'Neille, Mary. *Hailstones and Halibut Bones.* New York: Doubleday & Company, Inc., 1961.

Roberts, Clifton. *The Dot.* New York: Franklin, Watts, Inc., 1960.

Schaeffler, Ursula. *The Thief and the Blue Rose.* New York: Harcourt, Brace Jovanovich, Inc., 1969.

Schlein, Mirriam. *Shapes.* New York: William R. Scott, Inc., 1952.

Showers, Paul. *Find Out by Touching.* New York: William R. Scott, Inc., 1968.

Showers, Paul. *Follow Your Nose.* New York: Thomas Y. Crowell Company, 1969.

Stark, Karen. *My Tree.* Minneapolis: Carelrhoda Books, Inc., 1970.

Steiner, Charlotte. *Listen to My Seashell.* New York: Alfred A. Knopf, Inc., 1959.

Steiner, Charlotte. *My Bunny Feels Soft*. New York: Alfred A. Knopf, Inc., 1958.

Wise, Margaret Brown. *The Summer Noisy Book*. New York: Harper & Row Brothers, 1951. (Other books in this series are: *The Country Noisy Book, The Seashore Noisy Book,* and *The Quiet Noisy Book.*)

Films

Coronet, Coronet Building, 65 East South Water Street, Chicago, Illinois 60601
  My Five Senses (film strips and records)
  Learning With Your Ears (16mm)
  Learning With Your Eyes on the Way to School (16mm)

Encyclopedia Britannica Education Corp., 425 N. Michigan Avenue, Chicago, Illinois 60611
  The Better to See You
  The Better to Hear You
  The Smell of Things
  The Taste of Things
  The Feel of Things
  (film strips and records)

My Social Self

Beem, Lorraine and Jerold. *Two is a Team*. New York: Harcourt, Brace & Jovanovich, Inc., 1955.

Brown, Myra B. *Company's Coming for Dinner*. New York: Harper and Brothers, 1958.

Hoban, Russel C. *Nothing to Do*. New York: Harper & Row, 1964.
  Walter's father finally thinks of a way to keep his young son busy. Walter in turn discovers how to keep his baby sister busy in this humorous tale of a possum family.

Joslin, Sesyle. *What Do You Say, Dear?* New York: Harper and Brothers, 1958.

Schweitzer, Byrd Baylor. *Amigo*. New York: Macmillian, 1963.
  A story of a boy and a prairie dog puppy.

Schultz, Charles M. *I Need All the Friends I Can Get*. San Francisco, Calif.: Determined Productions, Inc., 1964.

Slobodkin, Lois. *One Is Good, But Two Are BETTER*. New York: Vanguard, 1956.

Stanek, Muriel. *About Our Class*. Westchester, Ill.: Benefic Press, 1968.
  Other Stanek books that are very colorful and appropriate for kindergarteners are: *I Am Here, My Family and I, My friends and I, Going to School, About Our School, I Can Do It.*

Udry, Janice. *Let's Be Enemies*. New York: Harper & Row, 1969.

Ylla and Bensall, Crosby. *Look Who's Talking*. New York: Harper & Row, 1962.
  An ostrich wants to be accepted by the group.

Zolotow, Charlotte. *Do You Know What I'll Do?* New York: Harper & Row, 1958.
  A little girl dreams about the many things she'll do for her baby brother when he grows up.

Zolotow, Charlotte. *My Friend John*. New York: Harper & Row, 1961.

Sources for Teachers

McAfee, Oralie. *The New Nursery School Learning Activities Booklets*. New York: General Learning Corp., 1969.

Shaftel, Fannie and George. *Words and Action—Role Playing Photo Problems for Young Children*. New York: Holt, Rinehart & Winston, Inc., 1967.

Staff. *Using Our Senses*. Minneapolis: University of Minnesota, 1967.

Focus on Self Development. (Teacher's Guide) Chicago: Science Research Associates, Inc., 1970.

Learning About the World. (Teacher's Guide) Boston: Allyn & Bacon, Inc., 1970.

Curriculum Guide for Kindergarten. Brighton, Colorado: District 27J, 1966.

Index